Barilla

I LOVE PASTA

AN ITALIAN LOVE STORY IN 100 RECIPES

The Taunton Press

EDITED BY
ACADEMIA BARILLA

FOREWORD
GUIDO, LUCA AND PAOLO BARILLA

PREFACE
MASSIMO MONTANARI

INTRODUCTION
GIANLUIGI ZENTI

HISTORY TEXTS
GIANCARLO GONIZZI

FOOD TEXTS
MARIAGRAZIA VILLA

RECIPES BY
CHEF MARIO GRAZIA
CHEF MARCELLO ZACCARIA

PHOTOGRAPHS
ALBERTO ROSSI
CHEF MARCELLO ZACCARIA
CHEF STEFANO LODI

ACADEMIA BARILLA EDITORIAL COORDINATION
CHATO MORANDI
CHIARA PISANO
ILARIA ROSSI

GRAPHIC DESIGN CLARA ZANOTTI

We ♥ Pasta

Barilla was born with pasta...as were we.

Our grandmother's kitchen led seamlessly into the pasta factory. The scent from the production lines filled our rooms and the entire neighborhood; it was warm, maternal, and reminiscent of wheat and countryside.

For us, pasta represents our roots, our family and our very identity.

It is wonderful to see pasta evolve and to be able to acknowledge it, day after day, as an eternal food, a food for everyone—the food of today and tomorrow. It has an age-old history that has undergone continuous renewal through the generations, by breaking down geographical and even cultural boundaries.

It is impossible not to love pasta. Its perfection lies in its simplicity: at its most elemental, made only of wheat flour and water, pasta carries all the flavor and energy of the marriage of earth and sun. Healthy and affordable, pasta unites families and people of all ages, in humble kitchens and sophisticated restaurants alike.

Italy boasts more than 300 pasta shapes. Every city has its own version, with its own special name, and a recipe for each shape, with thousands of variations according to tradition, season, geography, and local climate. Fish, vegetables, and herbs such as oregano, mint, and wild fennel, for example, prevail in the south, while cheese and meat reign in the north. It would be impossible to sum up the varieties of this cultural and culinary heritage in a few lines, or in a cookbook or even an entire encyclopedia, because pasta is a living thing. It evolves with the times and with the imagination of the cook.

It is this very variety, this incredible ability to adapt to different ingredients in potentially endless flavor combinations, that makes pasta such a special and modern food. Pasta may be Italian, but it belongs to the world.

Our dream today is to bring pasta into every corner of the globe, and for every single person to find his or her perfect pasta dish. More than a dream, it is a belief, which now has given rise to this book. This is a collection of recipes designed to promote knowledge and enjoyment of pasta, yet also to guide people in the discovery of this genuine pleasure through authentic Italian recipes enriched with ideas to suit local tastes: pasta and feijoada in Brazil, pasta and meatballs in the United States, and more ...because everyone loves pasta, and because pasta can be adapted to everyone's taste.

Guido, Luca, and Paolo Barilla

PAOLO BARILLA / *PASTA 24/7*

"The pasta is on the table," for me, is practically a theme song that has marked my family's daily meals since childhood.

Times and circumstances have changed, but pasta—my all-time favorite food—has always been with me, my constant companion. It provides ultimate gastronomic pleasure when prepared by a top chef, or a deep personal satisfaction when prepared just for myself or for a few friends; and it is always a reliable source of energy from the early morning hours through a long day of sports ahead.

My love for pasta ranges from its flavor to its nutritional and emotional value, all of which make this dish so much more than just food: it is a faithful point of reference that continues to serve as a leitmotif throughout my family history, my work, and my well-being. *BEST LOVED PASTA SHAPE: SPAGHETTI N° 5*

LUCA BARILLA / *MY WELLNESS CENTER*

Life is full of excitement, surprises, and unexpected changes. The business, the meetings, the family—each with its share of emotions, decisions, and responsibilities. Since I was born, however, there has been one constant in my life: the daily lunch around the table. It is a chance to catch up with the family, share a moment together, and enjoy a delicious plate of pasta ... always a guarantee of taste, health, and pleasure. It will forever be my source of well-being. *BEST LOVED PASTA SHAPE: CASARECCE*

GUIDO BARILLA / *EXPERIMENTATION WITHIN THE FAMILY RITUAL*

Pasta is a dish for kings and paupers alike. Its simplicity and its variety make it unique, and a pleasure to be discovered day after day. As such, it is the star of my daily family ritual.

Every opportunity to meet around the table becomes a time of experimentation: ranking our favorite shapes and choosing the best pasta/sauce combinations are forms of our never-ending exercise and play. Once again, pasta acts as the link between generations, strewn with the emotions of our lifelong memories. *BEST LOVED PASTA SHAPE: FUSILLI*

PASTA AS FOODSTUFF

Professor
MASSIMO MONTANARI

PAGE 6 / The Barilla shop in Cremona in 1949.

Although an ancient invention, pasta took many years to find a proper place at the table. Centuries ago, the Mediterranean diet was based on two different uses of cereal flour: it was mixed with water and cooked in the dry heat of the oven or of a hot surface (the model on which bread, pizza, and focaccia are based), or prepared dry and cooked in the moist heat of water (such as polenta). The basic principle of ancient dietetics, on which cooking practices were based, was the search for balance between the quality of foods, classified according to the oppositions hot/cold and dry/wet. The idea of balancing dry and wet supported the use of the oven (dry) for wet mixtures and of boiling (wet) for dry flours. Pasta struggled to find its place within this system, as its flour-water mixture fell into the first category, while its cooking method (boiling) fell into the second.

It took the invention of dry pasta to make the idea of a mixture cooked in water or stock conceivable. This, however, only occurred in the Middle Ages, when the practice of drying pasta—generatty a Middle Eastern custom—spread throughout the West, especially in Italy, as a result of the Muslim conquest of Sicily. In 1152, the geographer Idrisi reported that at

Trabia, near Palermo, "they produce an abundance of pasta that is exported extensively, to Calabria and to other countries, both Muslim and Christian, in great shiploads."

This eyewitness report also underscores the role of pasta as an industrial product: when it is dried, it can be preserved, stored, and transported with ease. From the twelfth century onward, pasta appeared among the foods consumed by traveling sailors and sold in the markets of port cities such as Genoa, Bari, and Naples. This introduced a new chapter in the history of pasta. It was no longer regarded as a sporadic and occasional food among many (as it was in ancient Roman times), but rather a genre in its own right, a food destined to become increasingly complex and codified. Over time, this genre became more focused, with many different shapes developing, each with its own particular name. Stuffed pasta (another medieval invention) also enjoyed great success.

An additional reason for the triumph of pasta was its inclusion in the category of "lean foods" that could replace meat on the many days when ecclesiastical legislation forbade its consumption. One of the oldest pasta lists appears in a 1636 text by Paolo Zacchia and dedicated to lenten foods, in which the author states: "There are many different types, some dry and some fresh; some thick and some thin; some made with wheat flour and some with other ingredients. They come in many different shapes; some are round, like those we call vermicelli or macaroni, some of which are hollow and others aren't; others are wide and straight, like lasagna; others are small and round, such as those we call millefanti; others are flat and narrow, in the shape of ribbons, commonly known as tagliolini; others are short and thick, called agnolini; others longer and thicker, referred to as gnocchi; and then there are a thousand other shapes, all of which are equally good and healthy."

The real turning point came in Naples, where, for the first time, pasta (until then considered a specialty food) became a means of sustenance for the city's population. This came about as a result of several factors. First, vast segments of the population lacked traditional resources (meat and vegetables), because of the economic difficulties suffered under Spanish rule; second, pasta became inexpensive, resulting from a number of inventions (such as the mechanical mixer and the bronze die) that made it more economical to produce. Originally in Naples, and then in many other cities and regions of southern Italy, pasta became, for many, the food par excellence, the mainstay of their daily diet. In the nineteenth century, this eating habit spread north, thanks also to Pellegrino Artusi, who, in his cookbook of 1891, introduced pasta as a "national" food. Meanwhile, a crowd of emigrants spread the image of Italian "macaroni eaters" worldwide, promoting the product internationally and encouraging the development abroad of pasta making and selling.

During the second half of the twentieth century, the boom of the so-called Mediterranean diet gave new international prestige to the product, elevating its image and shifting the focus onto quality.

PASTA, AN AMAZING CONJURING TRICK

GIANLUIGI ZENTI

Director of Academia Barilla

Pasta is a never-ending joy. Due to its versatility—enabled by its countless shapes and the equal bounty of sauces with which it can be served—pasta may be regarded as a veritable conjuring trick. Simply change an element, however small, such as the curvature of a shape or the herb of a sauce, and everything changes. Simply change a step in the method of preparation or a detail in the cooking technique, and everything changes. Simply change the way you dish up and serve it—for example, spreading the sauce on the bottom rather than using it as a topping, and, again, everything changes. In short, pasta is a masterpiece of magic: simple but always capable of arousing great wonder, not only for the palate, but for all the senses.

Like any self-respecting conjuring trick, however, pasta is also backed by technique. First, each shape goes best with a particular type of sauce, and should not be paired indiscriminately with just any condiment. Not surprisingly, in Italian cuisine a pasta dish is not determined by the sauce alone but by its successful match with a particular pasta variety. In general, the lighter, less structured shapes, such as farfalle, are best paired with fresh fish or vegetable condiments. More complex shapes, like *tortiglioni* and *bucatini*, go best with

structured toppings, like meat *ragùs* or an Amatriciana sauce. Large shapes, such as *paccheri* and *ziti*, are ideal with sauces that combine elegance and texture, while the most uncomplicated, everyday shapes, such as *mezze maniche*, are suitable for quick and easy condiments. Pastas with porous or ribbed surfaces absorb thin sauces best, while those with a smooth texture are perfect with enveloping condiments. Egg pasta, on the other hand, is excellent with sauces based on butter, milk, or cream, while semolina varieties are delicious with leaner, less creamy sauces.

For the very reason that each pasta has its own ideal sauce, Academia Barilla —an international center dedicated to the dissemination of Italian gastronomic culture—wishes to highlight the extraordinary richness of pasta, to which every region of Italy has contributed over the centuries. The Barilla "Le Regionali" product line offers the most popular and widespread pasta varieties, such as *orecchiette* from Puglia, *trofie* from Liguria, *casarecce* from Sicily, and *reginette* from Naples. Because the magic of Italian pasta is not limited to *spaghetti*, *penne rigate*, or *fusilli*. There is no end to the varieties that can be pulled out of the hat.

CONTENTS

LONG PASTA *PAGE 32*

SHORT PASTA PAGE 84

BAKED AND EGG PASTA *PAGE 188*

SOUP PASTA *PAGE 242*

THE NAME OF PASTA

since 1877

(Images: Barilla Historical Archives, Parma)

The HISTORY THAT CONNECTS BARILLA WITH WHEAT IS TRULY EXCEPTIONAL: PARMA RECORDS FROM 1576 ATTEST TO THE EXISTENCE OF A MASTER BAKER, OVIDIUS BARILLA, AN ANCESTOR OF THE FAMILY WHO, AT THE TURN OF THE NINETEENTH CENTURY, BREATHED LIFE—IN WHAT IS NOW RIGHTLY CONSIDERED THE ITALIAN FOOD VALLEY—INTO A COMPANY DESTINED TO BECOME A UNIVERSAL LEADER OF PASTA AND A CHAMPION OF ITALIAN FLAVOR WORLDWIDE.

Barilla owes its origins to a bakery opened in 1877 by Pietro Barilla, Senior (1845–1912), in Parma, on Strada Vittorio Emanuele. The company's history is marked by a steady and progressive growth. In 1910, the plant was built in Barriera Vittorio Emanuele, fitted with the era's most cutting-edge machinery. Pietro was succeeded by his sons, Gualtiero (1881–1919) and Riccardo (1880–1947). After Gualtiero's untimely death in 1919, Riccardo managed the company until 1947 with his wife, Virginia, keeping the company abreast with the latest technologies and transforming it into one of the most important regional pasta factories in Italy.

After the Second World War, Riccardo's sons, Pietro (1913–1993) and Gianni (1917–2004), laid the groundwork for the strong growth enjoyed during the fifties with the construction of the new plant in Via Veneto in 1957 and the testing of continuous production lines, and the sixties, with the construction of the breadstick and rusks factory in Rubbiano in 1965 and of the Pedrignano factory in 1969, still today the largest pasta-processing plant in the world.

PAGES 16-17 / Group photo of the Barilla factory workers in a 1921 shot by Fratelli Zambini.
Riccardo Barilla can be seen sitting in the front row, with his hands on his lap.
Above, a large sign with the corporate brand, designed by Ettore Vernizzi and registered in 1910.

PAGE 18 / The Barilla complex in a 1927 shot by Alberto Montacchini. On the left, the pasta factory with its chimney stack is clearly visible. On the right, another chimney stack marks the furnaces.

The experience gained during his trip to America in 1951 gave Pietro Barilla, who had been working in the family business since 1936, a thorough insight into the guiding principles underlying his work in several areas. He oversaw technological innovation, with the testing of continuous production cycles, which would significantly raise product quality and the plants' production capacity; hygienic packaging and the renewed distribution network; and the importance of investing in advertising, causing the company to move, in the short span of a decade, from a regional to a national concern.

The successful collaboration with several members of the Italian cultural scene contributed significantly to defining the company's global corporate image. After completely overhauling and expanding the factory in Via Veneto (now Viale Barilla) so as to reach a production output of about 1,320,000 pounds of pasta a day, strong market demand caused the company to abandon the idea of expanding further in the same area, which became-considered inadequate for their needs. Therefore, in the 1940s, Barilla began to plan its

PAGE 19 / The Barilla pasta factory, here in a 1964 photograph, was entirely rebuilt by Gian Luigi Giordani after the war, with ribbon windows and a covered surface area of over 24.000 square meters.

move to Pedrignano, near the Autostrada del Sole motorway. In 1960, at the peak of the "economic miracle," Barilla became a joint stock company, thus completing a decade of significant transformations.

In 1970, Gianni and Pietro Barilla sold the business to the American multinational company Grace. However, in 1979, after several attempts, Pietro managed to regain a majority stake in the company, which he presided over, bringing it to unimagined levels of growth and fame. Under his leadership, a new technological overhaul was started, with the construction of new production lines and facilities, and the launch of important communication campaigns. Pietro, ever a generous benefactor, donated to the University of Parma the seat of the Faculty of Engineering (1987). Furthermore, he put together a remarkable collection of art, which he exhibited publicly in 1993, to mark his eightieth birthday. He also donated to Parma a fountain sculpted by Pietro Cascella (1921–2008), to be installed in one of the city's squares (1994).

PAGE 20 / The monumental Barilla pasta factory in Parma, built along the Milano-Bologna highway, with the art works *Disco solare*, by Arnaldo Pomodoro, and *Cavallo*, by Mario Ceroli. In the background, the mill and the large flour silos featuring the corporate brand.

With Pietro's death, in 1993, his sons—Guido, Luca, and Paolo—assumed the helm of the family business, carrying out a major interior reshuffle and expanding on the international market.

At this time, the company acquired the pasta factories Misko (1991), in Greece; Filiz (1994), in Turkey; and Yemina and Vesta (2001), in Mexico, and built the first Italian-owned plant for the production of pasta on American soil, opened in Ames, Iowa, on June 25, 1999—a success replicated in 2007 with the plant in Avon, New York.

On the threshold of the new millennium, Barilla had become the world leader in pasta and the leading business in Europe for bakery products under the brands Mulino Bianco (since 1976) and Wasa (since 1999). The Barilla group also owns the pasta brand Voiello (since 1975) and the bakery brand Pavesi (since 1992).

PAGE 21 / The square leading onto the Barilla offices in Parma, designed by the architect Vico Magistretti, with the steel sculpture *Il nodo* by the contemporary artist Giuliano Vangi.

Established as a simple bread and pasta shop more than 130 years ago, Barilla is today the leading Italian food group in the world: it has 25 factories (20 in Italy and 5 abroad) and directly manages 6 mills that supply 70 percent of the raw materials it requires. Always geared toward customer satisfaction and respect for health and nature, the Barilla brand has established itself in the world mainly due to the quality of its products, resulting from considerable investments in research, innovation, and technology, and from a profound respect for both raw materials and consumers, in line with Pietro Barilla's motto: "Give the people what you would give your children."

It is no wonder that Barilla was founded in Parma, a land that has made food its mission. Here, a small pasta factory of yesteryear has become one of the ambassadors of Italian cuisine in the world.

PASTA TECHNOLOGY:
GIVING SHAPE TO FLAVOR

GIANCARLO GONIZZI

Curator of Academia Barilla Gastronomic Library

ARCHITECTURE FOR THE MOUTH

Taste has its own strict rules, deeply intertwined with the tools that Mother Nature has given us. As a result, pasta takes on one flavor or another, based on its shape and its ability to absorb the sauce.

In cooking, as in architecture, the most important artistic expressions lie in three-dimensional objects, and, indeed, pasta may be defined as architecture for the mouth.

Through the mouth, the mind receives information on shape, surface, and texture, as well as on scent, taste, and temperature. It enables us to discern differences in all types of pasta, and their individual characteristics are revealed. For these characteristics to be detected in the mouth, it is essential for the pasta to be *al dente*.

The enormous variety of available shapes is much more than a pleasant form of entertainment for the mouth. These very shapes often denote a common origin of pasta and of those who eat it. In a way, they identify an entire people, a land, a country. From a historical point of view, just as brickwork did for architecture, pasta ushered in a new era in cookery and in regional and national pride

THE SHAPES OF TASTE

Originally, pasta making was done by hand, with a good dose of elbow grease. Therefore, because the dough was shaped by hand or flattened into a thin sheet and cut into strips of varying widths (just as homemade pasta is today), the only shapes possible were gnocchi, tagliatelle, tagliolini, fettuccine, and the like.

Spaghetti, at least in the West, was achieved with the advent of machinery (in particular, of extruders), as were all the other shapes that, over time, have enriched the varied world of pasta. There are hundreds of different shapes to suit all tastes, the evolution of which we will attempt to outline by following a brief history of the technological progress that has affected this most versatile of foods.

PAGE 23 / Interior of an eighteenth-century pasta factory in a plate
from *Encyclopédie* by Diderot and D'Alembert.

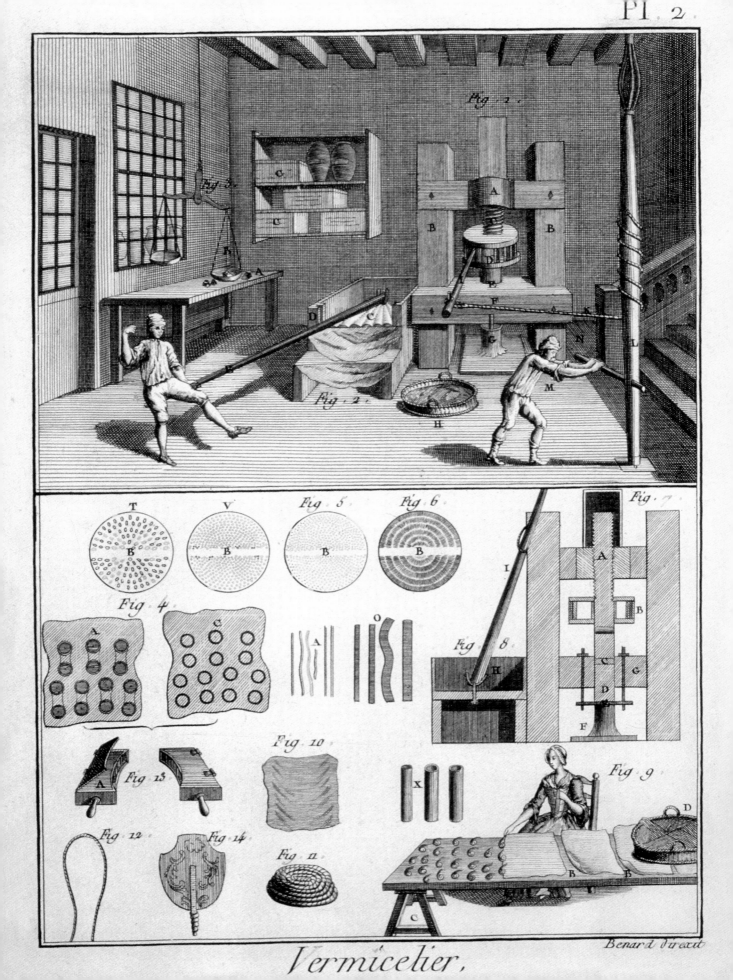

PI. 2

Vermicelier.

Benard direxit.

ORIGINAL SHAPES

Gnocchi, the forefather of all pasta, soon evolved into other shapes obtained by manipulating the dough by hand or using very simple tools, mixing wheat and water to produce numerous local variants, such as *trofie* from Recco, *orecchiette* and *cavatieddi* from Puglia, and many more.

It was later realized that by exerting pressure on the mixture and rolling it with a smooth, uniform stick, you could get a thin sheet of pastry. Roman lasagna, initially fried and later boiled, came first, followed by a host of similar shapes, which were distinguished by two linguistic roots.

In Central Europe, where a strictly egg-based form of pastry had developed independently, the Latin *nodellus* gave rise to nouilles in France, *nudeln* in Germany, and *noodles* in English. In Italy, two tailoring terms were taken as points of reference: "cut" (*taglio*), resulting in *tagliatelle*, tagliolini, and *taglierini*, and "ribbon" (*fettuccia*), giving rise to *fettucce* and fettuccine. All are delicious to eat, or *pappare* in dialect: hence, the *pappardelle* of Tuscany and the *paparelle* of Verona and the Veneto region. Pastry also lies at the origin of short pasta, such as *farfalle* (*stricchetti* in Emilia Romagna), *garganelli* (rectangles of dough wrapped around a stick and ridged), and the magnificent *corzetti* from the coast west of Genoa, known as the Riviera di Ponente: medallions pressed between two engraved wooden "stamps," which convert the disks into veritable bas-reliefs featuring flowers, stars, olive branches, and human profiles.

PAGE 24 / Bronze and copper dies for the production of *bucatini*, *ziti*, and *spaghetti*.

THE DIE: FRUIT OF SKILL AND CREATIVITY

The step from a closed mold to a perforated model is but a short one. Thus, the principle that gave birth to the simple tool for the preparation of homemade *passatelli* was transferred, with the help of a mechanical press, to dies, the large molds used to shape pasta.

Die makers, capable of drilling absolutely identical holes in the metal disk that closed the presses and shaped the pasta, were extremely skilled and full of imagination. The principle was very easy to apply to pasta factories: At a simple change of the die, a new pasta shape was ready to be dried—with the aid of the air and sun of southern Italy and Liguria—and then packaged and shipped.

The first dies were made of copper, but these were soon replaced by bronze ones, which were much more durable and longer lasting. Moreover, bronze enabled the creation of smoother and more precise holes, two essential elements for optimal drying and cooking, as even a small difference in the thickness of pasta affected the quality of the final dish. Bronze dies, while smoother, were also more compact than copper, giving the pasta uniform porosity, a quality still greatly appreciated by gourmets today.

In the twentieth century, steel dies with bronze or Teflon inserts came into widespread use, so as to withstand the high pressures of the ultramodern continuous production lines.

PASTA PREPARATION STAGES

Dies were the last stage of a technological evolution that, from the eleventh to the sixteenth centuries, saw the succession of various eras in pasta making—with the establishment of the guild of the Fidelari in Genoa in 1574 and in Savona in 1577, and of the Vermicellari in Naples in 1579 and in Palermo in 1605—and the easing of human labor by means of increasingly large machines and tools for use in workshops.

Specific machinery was developed for each of the four essential steps in pasta production: mixing the ingredients, kneading the dough, shaping the pasta, drying the pasta, and, finally, packaging the product.

MIXING THE INGREDIENTS

The flour obtained from grounding durum wheat was first screened and sifted to remove any impurities, and then mixed with water in a large container—the mixer—fitted with mechanical arms. The machine was usually elevated, enabling the dough to be tilted into the kneading machine placed below it.

PAGE 25 / Mechanical dough mixer manufactured by the company
Ceschina, Busi & C. of Brescia in the late 19th century.

PAGE 26 / The engine room of the Barilla pasta factory, with the continuous Braibanti presses installed in 1938.

PAGE 27 TOP / The Barilla factory kneading hall in a 1913 picture by Luigi Vaghi.

KNEADING THE DOUGH

As durum wheat flour is vitreous by nature, it doesn't absorb water easily, making further processing required. The mixture is "massaged" so as to enable the water to penetrate the dough evenly, making it smooth and even. To obtain this result, kneading troughs were first used, often operated by several men. These were later replaced by stone mills driven by hydraulic force, rudimentary kneading machines operated by wooden paddles, and, finally, the widespread and effective motor-operated kneaders with metal conical rollers. After kneading, the mixture was transferred manually to the next processing phase. In some cases, especially for egg pasta, this consisted of rolling out the dough to an even thickness by passing the mixture between smooth rollers. This is because, in the early days, shaping took place using thin sheets of pastry.

PAGE 27 BOTTOM RIGHT / Vertical screw press for the production of long pasta, Italy, nineteenth century.

SHAPING THE PASTA

In the fifteenth century, the technique of extrusion molding began to take hold, thanks to the use of the screw press, first recorded in 1548 in a text by Cristoforo da Messisbugo, carver at the Court of Ferrara, and then by Bartolomeo Scappi, chef to Pope Pius V, in 1570. These tools were initially made of wood, with only the extruder being made of bronze, while in the nineteenth century cast-iron versions were produced, significantly increasing their size and yield. Dies with different sized and shaped holes were fitted in the opening, enabling variously shaped pastas to be produced. These were then cut manually by the pasta maker, or mechanically by means of a rotary knife placed outside the die. Horizontal presses were used mainly for short soup pastas, while vertical ones were used to produce long pastas. Spaghetti—the Eastern noodle is an independent version—were modeled by hand. It is only through Italian inventiveness and technology that—with the aid of appropriate machinery, gradually improved with the application of hydraulic force—hundreds of different pasta shapes were developed.

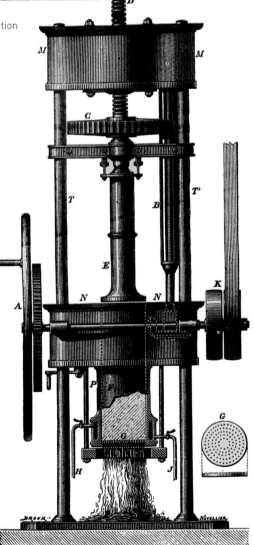

PAGE 28 TOP / Spaghetti production around Naples in the 1920s.
The outdoor drying of spaghetti is favored by the regular and intermittent sea breezes typical of the area.

PAGE 28 CENTER / Short pasta static dryers at a Barilla pasta factory in a 1932 photo.

PAGE 28 BOTTOM / The Barilla shop on Strada Vittorio Emanuele in 1927, with special pasta drawers and blown-glass vases from the Toso glassworks in Murano, displaying the various pasta shapes for sale.

DRYING THE PASTA

The freshly shaped pasta was then either laid out on wide nets (short cuts) or hung on canes (long cuts) to dry, an essential phase in order to ensure the product retained its firmness while cooking. A preliminary pre-drying phase called *incartamento* (from the Italian term *carta*, or "paper," since upon drying, the surface would whiten and resemble sheets of paper) was followed by a period of tempering in a cool environment, in order to redistribute the internal humidity. A final, static, drying phase was then carried out, either outdoors or in a ventilated place. Later, this phase was conducted in rooms fitted with fans and heating systems. The drying phase, meticulously performed by a master pasta maker, was particularly delicate, since the parameters could vary based on the season, the climate, the presence of wind, and from one pasta factory to another.

PACKAGING THE PASTA

At this point the pasta was ready to be shipped, either in baskets made of chestnut bark and lined with paper, or in wooden boxes or cotton bags, weighed one by one. Once it reached its destination by sea or rail, the shopkeeper would remove the pasta from its packaging (which had to be returned to the pasta factory) and arrange it in a large chest of drawers or in attractive glass jars, ready to be sold, loose, to customers, wrapped in typically light blue food-safe paper parcels.

PAGE 29 / Modern continuous production lines in the Barilla Pedrignano plant (Parma), inaugurated in 1970.

PRODUCTION AUTOMATION

In the early twentieth century, many attempts were made to automate the various stages of production, to reduce waste and downtime, and to increase the hygiene and quality of the end product.

In 1917, Féréol Sandragné from France had the idea of applying a technology used for the production of bricks to the process of pasta making, patenting a continuous press in which a long continuous screw kneaded the dough. In 1933, the engineers Giuseppe and Mario Braibanti, sons of a pasta maker from Parma, managed to combine the kneader and press into a single machine, so as to avoid interrupting the production process. It wasn't until the 1950s that, after several years of experimentation, the Barilla plant in Parma developed a technology to automate the drying phase by moving the pasta on belts or canes inside long dryers calibrated so as to alternate various stages of drying and tempering. In 1955, Pietro Barilla decided to abandon the old system of shipping pasta in boxes or bags, and launched the modern process of packaging it in individual cardboard boxes of standard weight. The color chosen for the Barilla packaging was the light blue of the food-safe paper the consumers had long been used to, a decision that has inextricably tied the brand to the color blue, which has taken on an increasingly dark hue over the years.

SO, HOW MANY PASTA SHAPES ARE THERE?

How many types of pasta were invented by the die makers? By analyzing several old pasta catalogs, it is evident that somewhere between 250 to 300 shapes were offered. The easiest and most spontaneous way of categorizing pasta is into long, short, and soup shapes. Then, there are two parallel categories: rolled pasta (the factory version of homemade pastry) and stuffed pasta.

Long pasta can be further split into two types: cylindrical, either solid or hollow, and rectangular or "rounded." The first group includes some forebears, such as vermicelli and spaghetti, with their smaller (*spaghettini*, *vermicellini*) and larger (*spaghettoni*, *vermicelloni*) versions as well as evocatively named shapes, such as *capelli d'angelo* ("angel hair"), *capellini* ("thin hair"), *bucatini* (from bucato, or "pierced"), *perciatelli* (perhaps from the Neapolitan term *pertusio*, or "hole"), *ziti* or *zitoni*, traditionally served at weddings (*zita* means "bride-to-be"), and *mezzanelli* ("intermediate in size" between big bucatini and half zita). "Rectangular" shapes are an industrial adaptation of long tagliatelle, with the flat varieties becoming *linguine*, *bavette*, *tagliarelli*, and *lasagnette*. The most famous shape in this category is the Ligurian *trenette*, similar in shape to shoelaces (called *trenette* in the Genoese dialect), to which it also owes its name. The wavy forms of *fettuccine* create a special "long pasta" category unto themselves: originally called *lasagne ricce*, they were then dedicated to the wife of the King of Italy on her visit to Naples, becoming known as "reginette" (from *regina*, or "queen").

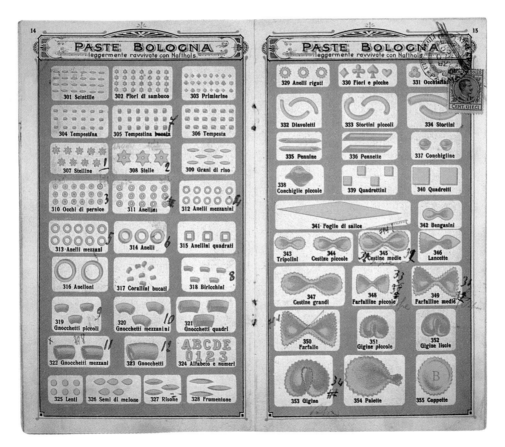

PAGE 30 / The Barilla product catalog from 1916, with a wide range of short pastas.

PAGE 31 / Drawing of the *marille* pasta designed by Giorgetto Giugiaro for the Voiello pasta factory in 1983.

CURRENT AFFAIRS AND IMAGINATION, THE ORIGINS OF PASTA NAMES

Short pastas are the most entertaining element of the category as a whole, as many of their names and shapes have been influenced by their times. At the end of the nineteenth century, *ditalini rigati* were also known as *garibaldini* as a tribute to Garibaldi, one of Italy's forefathers. Perhaps it was in honor of the Princess Mafalda of Savoy (or the daughter of a pasta maker) that *fettuccelle ricce* became known as *mafalde* and *mafaldine*, also known as *tripoline* and *bengasine* to mark the Italian colony in Libya. Similarly, the landing in the Bay of Assab, on the Red Sea, in 1882, gave the green light to *assabesi* (large shells) and, shortly thereafter, to the similar but smaller *abissini*. *Chinesi* and *chinesini* (shells) had already existed for some time, while, in the 1930s, Art Deco influenced the creation of *radiatori*, *pulegge*, and *ingranaggi*.

After the Second World War, in the 1950s, new avenues were explored, with the *dischi volanti* (flying saucers), followed by floral, celebratory, and figurative pastas.

In 1983, the prestigious Voiello pasta factory of Torre Annunziata launched an innovative undertaking, entrusting the Turin industrial designer Giorgetto Giugiaro with the task of creating a new shape, the *marille*, which resembled an ocean wave and enjoyed considerable press coverage.

In 1987, it was Barilla's turn to launch an entire line of new shapes: the *Esclusivi* line, stemming from the design and experience of the die maker Carlo Mori, introduced the *bifore*, with the profile of the Barilla "B," the *trifogli*, spaghetti with three grooves that speed up cooking, the *nicchiole*, excellent for absorbing sauce and inspired by the shape of mushrooms, and the *castellane*, refined ribbed shells that go perfectly with cheese and vegetable sauces.

And now there is the electronic age and the spread of the Internet, which has given rise to the latest pasta shape: An Italian pasta factory has patented an "@", the at sign used in e-mail addresses, to be served with a Bolognese sauce, preferably far from the computer.

Giugiaro Design

PASTA IS SERVED

Italian-style pasta dishes, in all their countless variations, are homemade creations based on a special blend of local resources (wheat, eggs, vegetables, fish, seafood, meat, cheese) and popular ingenuity, frequently resulting in nutritionally complete recipes. Not surprisingly, pasta is often considered a meal unto itself, enabling simplified, time-saving meals. wherever you are—at home or at the restaurant, at work or with friends—pasta is always sure to be a pleasure, spiced with the age-old culinary experience and imagination of Italy. It's an ever-new way of giving shape to flavor.

LONG PASTA

THE MOST POETIC

I ♥ Pasta

Long pasta, with its gentle waves, its voluptuous coils, and its creative tangles, is the most evocative and poetic of pastas. It conjures distant memories and ancient traditions revisited in a modern key. It warms the heart and awakens the taste buds with its continuous, seemingly infinite shapes, evoking the joyous freedom of forgotten childhood emotions. Long pasta is a pleasure for all the senses.

Yet, for long pasta to best express its poetic qualities and create a composition of rhythm, symmetry, and correspondence, it must pair with the right sauce. This is as fundamental for long shapes—whether round, square, rectangular, or flat, or, again, nested or coiled—as it is for any other type of pasta. A robust sauce such as carbonara, for example, one of the flagship recipes of Italian cuisine, is not suitable for the ultrafine capelli d'angelo or capellini, but ideal with thicker types, such as spaghetti. Likewise, an important long pasta such as Neapolitan ziti (a dialect term for "bride and groom," because they were once enjoyed solely at weddings) would be lost on a light garlic, oil, and chile-pepper sauce, better suited to thinner, non-hollow shapes such as spaghettini or vermicelli. And if you really want to prepare ziti with a simple tomato sauce, better to bake them au gratin, sprinkled with breadcrumbs, to make the recipe more festive.

Some of Italy's most traditional long pastas have come to be identified with certain classic sauces. The Amatriciana sauce, for example, another mainstay of the Italian gastronomic tradition, is traditionally prepared with bucatini, a long, hollow shape typical of Rome. Pesto or vegetable and fish sauces, instead, are often served with bavette, a rectangular and slightly convex spaghetti-like pasta native to Genoa.

BAVETTE

SERVED MAINLY DRY, COMBINED WITH SIMPLE OIL OR BUTTER, FISH OR CLAM SAUCES, AND PESTO.

While widespread throughout Italy, they are typical of Liguria, where numerous recipes are based on this type of pasta. The larger version is more popular in southern Italy.

This pasta, which comes in narrow, thin strips, takes its name from the Italian term *bava* ("burr"). In the 1863 *Dictionary* published by Pietro Fanfani, they are cited as "long, thin soup pasta," also known as *baverine*. They come in different sizes: small, medium and large. They have a variety of names depending on the shape and region of use, and are also called *fettuccelle*, *lingue di passero*, *linguine*, *pappardelle* and *trenette*. In Sicily, they are known as lasagneddi.

Bavette *is a very old type of pasta, the name of which perhaps derives from the French term baverette, documented in Provence from as early as the thirteenth century. Originally from Liguria, and Genoa in particular, this pasta is characterized by a flattened, biconvex section, providing a greater surface to absorb the sauce, whether pesto or other sauces made with mortar and pestle, or even a simple combination of cheese and oil or melted butter. On* the palate, the bavette's greater surface allows the taste buds to more intensely experience the seasonings.

Often confused with *linguine, bavette is traditionally served with pesto. Pesto is certainly the most typical and famous regional Italian sauce, with basil as its main ingredient. Its name derives from the pounding action, referred to as pestare in Italian, traditionally performed in a marble mortar. In its preparation, fresh baby basil leaves and garlic are combined with coarse sea salt (which helps crush the basil in the mortar) and delicately sweet Ligurian extra-virgin olive oil—another excellent product of the region—so as not to overpower the aroma, as well as pine nuts and aged Parmigiano Reggiano and Pecorino cheeses.*

LONG DURUM WHEAT PASTA
Average size:
length 255.00 mm • width 3.10 mm • thickness 1.32 mm

BUCATINI

DRY, TRADITIONALLY SERVED WITH THE AMATRICIANA SAUCE OR WITH BACON, VEGETABLE, CHEESE, AND EGG SAUCES.

While widespread in Liguria and in central-southern Italy, bucatini is typical of Lazio, especially in the area of Amatrice.

Its meaning, which is evident in the Italian language, derives from the small *buco* (or "hole") in the middle that characterizes its structure. It is also known by different names in different regions of Italy: *fidelini* in Liguria, *perciatelli* or *candele* in Campania, and *ziti* or *agoni bucati* in Sicily.

Pasta col pertuso, *that is, "pasta with a hole," is mentioned as far back as 1630 by the Neapolitan writer Giambattista Basile (1575–1633) in the collection of stories entitled* Cunto de li Cunti (Tale of Tales).
The Amatriciana sauce takes its name from Amatrice, an ancient town in central Italy, now in the province of Rieti, inhabited since prehistoric times and later built up by the Romans, and set in a green valley bordering the four regions of Lazio, Umbria, Marche, and Abruzzo.
The recipe, invented by shepherds, was essentially made with pork jowl (guanciale), Pecorino cheese, and pepper, the few ingredients available in the mountains and still used for preparing the pasta alla gricia, *and* was only ennobled with tomatoes in the late nineteenth century. It was during this period that, following the crisis suffered by the sheep-farming industry, many people from Amatrice—following in the footsteps of several cooks to the Popes—moved to Rome and found work in the restaurant business. The first historical restaurant specializing in dishes from Amatrice was opened in 1860, close to Piazza Navona, by Luigi Sagnotti, who helped to disseminate the dish in the capital, and then on a national scale.*

≪When choosing pasta, an Italian becomes a poet unbeknownst to himself. And when he greedily sucks in a plateful of bucatini, he becomes a musician, whistling like an upside down piffero.≫
From: Marchi, Cesare, *Quando siamo a tavola*, Milan (I), Rizzoli, 1990.

LONG, HOLLOW DURUM WHEAT PASTA
Average size:
length 255.00 mm • diameter 3.02 mm • thickness 0.90 mm

CAPELLINI

Liguria, Lazio, and as an industrial production, all regions of Italy.

Its meaning, which is evident in the Italian language, derives from capello, or "hair," due to its fineness. *Capellini* are also known as *capelvenere, maccheroni ciociari*, or *ramicc*ia in the Lazio region of Italy.

Mentioned in seventeenth-century Roman texts as a type of extremely thin egg pasta, capellini were among the specialties prepared in some of the city's convents and sent, in a curious ceremony, to new mothers and to ailing members of the noble families of Rome. In Naples, capelli d'angelo were used to prepare an oven-baked dish, while in some regions of southern Italy, these fine strands of pasta were used for a very special dessert.

The Roman historian Count Alessandro Moroni (1844–1915) describes the ceremony whereby the *capelli d'angelo*, prepared by nuns, were delivered to the pregnant women of noble Roman families to help, it was thought, milk production: ⟨⟨*...brought in by several carriers, one could see the towering 'pavilion of new mothers,' that is, a magnificent and bizarre construction entirely covered with long rows of tagliolini, capelli d'angelo, or other egg pastas, alternated by a swarm of capons and hens for the use of the illustrious new mother.*⟩⟩
From: Moroni, Alessandro, *Vie, voci e viandanti della vecchia Roma*, Rome (I), Unione Coop. Editrice, 1894.

LONG DURUM WHEAT PASTA.
THEY ALSO COME IN AN EGG VERSION
Average size:
length 255.00 mm • diameter 1.17 m

LASAGNETTE

DRY, WITH RICH MEAT SAUCES, BUT ALSO WITH VEGETABLES, CHEESE, AND CREAM.

All regions of Italy, but mainly in the center and the south.

This is a recent trade name clearly based on the term *lasagna* (see the relevant section). Over time, the name has been used for different types of pasta, also with different cooking methods. For the purposes of this book, we will take it to mean the industrially produced variety with smooth edges, often referred to as tagliatelle, or with curled edges, often known as *lasagne ricche* (curly *lasagna*), *reginette* ("little queens," probably for their resemblance to the scallops on top of a crown), or *mafaldine* (named after the Italian Princess Mafalda of Savoy [1902–1944], daughter of Victor Emmanuel III).

This is one of the oldest Italian pastas, consisting of a sheet of dough cut into different shapes and proportions, depending on the region. There are many records of its use in Roman times, in the Middle Ages, and during the Renaissance. The use of a toothed pasta cutter (or speronella*) dating back to the Etruscan era permitted*

the production of the curled variety even in ancient times.
This type of pasta was prepared with durum wheat flour in southern Italy, while in the north, which was climatically unsuitable for the cultivation of durum wheat, it was prepared with wheat flour and eggs, the latter an indispensable binder for the dough. Indeed, the greater presence of egg pasta in the north is due to the climate. This is why there are several examples of the same kind of pasta made with or without eggs, and with different names in different areas of use. These are all close relatives of the various types of tagliatelle.

LONG DURUM WHEAT PASTA MADE FROM A SHEET
OF DOUGH WRAPPED INTO THE SHAPE OF A NEST
Average size:
length 30.00 mm • thickness 0.90 mm

MACCHERONCINI

Southern Italy, but today all regions of Italy.

The term *macaroni*, a generic term for pasta, is interpreted differently in northern and southern Italy.

The word is thought to derive from the verb *ammaccare*, that is, "to beat forcefully", as happens when kneading the dough. In the south, the term is used for long and narrow pastas like *bavette*, while in the north it refers to short pasta tubes.

The oldest use of macaroni *is within funeral rites and wakes: the Greek word* macarioi, *meaning "blessed," was used to indicate the deceased, while* macarìa *was a broth served, as late as the sixteenth century, at funerals.*

Macco was also the name of a silly and naive character of the ancient Atellan comedies, and the term maccherone *is used in a document of 1041 to indicate a fool.*

In the Middle Ages, gnocchi, and indeed all kinds of pasta, were referred to as maccheroni, *probably from the term* ammaccare. *Indeed, the word is used with this meaning in a story of the Decameron by Boccaccio, in the idyllic description of the* Paese di Bengodi, *or the mythical land of plenty:* «*...and on a mountain, all of grated Parmesan cheese, dwell folk that do nought else but make macaroni and ravioli, and boil them in capon's broth...*» *(Book 8, chapter 3).*
The term mangiamaccheroni, *or "macaroni eaters," originally referred to the Sicilian population—the island has been documented as the leading region for the production of dry pasta since the twelfth century—while the Neapolitans, known as* mangiafoglie, *or "leaf eaters," due to their diet of cabbage and vegetables, only converted to pasta, for economic reasons, in the seventeenth century, soon becoming associated with the concept of assiduous pasta eaters. The traditional Neapolitan recipe involved boiling* macaroni *and flavoring them in the likeness of Vesuvius: black with ground pepper and white with grated cacio cheese (hence the saying come il* cacio sui maccheroni—*"like cacio [cheese] on macaroni"—to indicate a perfect match). Tomato wasn't paired with macaroni until the nineteenth century. Both the custom of preparing pasta on the streets of the city and the sometimes folkloric description of foreign travelers on their grand tour contributed to this pasta becoming inextricably linked with Naples and its surrounding territory.*

«THEATRICAL MACARONI
The monk Bernardino Stefonio, professor of Rhetoric at the Collegio Romano in the second half of the fifteenth century, wrote a mock-heroic poem in Latin called Macaroides, *a title that in itself reveals the intentions of the author. This poem, which is a true macaroni epic, speaks with ardor of a long war waged by the Sicilian pastas against the legumes of Tuscany, which ended with the victory of the former.*
In the wake of his poem, Stefonio created a play revolving around the various protagonists of "Maccaronis," making them behave like actors in a production in two acts, the Maccaronea. »
From: Sada, Luigi, *Spaghetti e Compagni*, Edizioni del Centro Librario, Biblioteca de "La Taberna", Bari (I), 1982, p. 44.

THE MUSICIAN GIACOMO ROSSINI AND MACARONI
«*Rossini's governess still lives in Paris. Her name is Ms. Giulia Barbenoire. She entered into his service at the age of 18 and never left the little house at Passy until she had closed her master's eyes. Every Saturday Rossini would hold one of his famous lunches; 15 place settings were always ready for anyone who wanted to come. Everyone was always thrilled with the famous macaroni Rossini prepared with his own hands, the recipe for which was handed down by the master to Jacopo Caponi."* And here it is:
"For the macaroni to be tasty, you must not only have good pasta, excellent butter, and superior tomato sauce and Parmigiano cheese, but also an intelligent person to cook, season, and serve them.»
From: "Il Popolo Romano", 10 marzo 1920.

I MACCHERONI E IL POMODORO
In 1913, Antonio Bizzozero, a pioneer in the modernization of agriculture in Parma, declared: "Rest assured that macaroni in tomato sauce and seasoned with butter of pure fresh cream and aged Parmesan cheese will become two institutions worldwide." *It is safe to say he was right.*
From: "Agricoltura parmense." Special issue of "L'Avvenire Agricolo." Parma (I), May 1937, p. 113.

LONG, HOLLOW DURUM WHEAT PASTA
Average size:
length 255.00 mm • diameter 4.50 mm • thickness 0.90 mm

SPAGHETTI / SPAGHETTINI

All regions of Italy.

The term clearly derives from the word *spago*, or "string," as a reference to the shape of the pasta. This was probably the first pasta to be produced with a die, perforated with simple cylindrical holes. The thinner versions are also referred to as *capelli d'angelo*, *capelvenere*, *fidelini*, *sopracapellini*, and *spaghettini*, and the thicker ones as *filatelli* and *spaghettoni*. It is interesting to note that there is no pasta known merely as *spago*, the neutral form of the word.

This is, without doubt, the best-known pasta shape and the most representative of Italian cuisine in the world. Pizza and spaghetti *still epitomize Italian culture for foreigners in their first encounter with Italy's culinary traditions.*
The first written report of a long pasta, known as vermicelli *and synonymous with* spaghetti, *dates back to the twelfth century. Even in that distant age, pasta traveled across the Mediterranean Sea, becoming widespread in the Italian ports and in the cities that then encouraged its spread to the inland regions of Italy.*
Spaghetti *could be found from Sicily to Sardinia, and in the ports of maritime cities such as Genoa, Amalfi, and Pisa. But it was in the Gulf of Naples that the greatest guild dedicated exclusively to pasta-making was established. Stemming from the guild of bakers and known as the* Arte dei Vermicellai, *the association soon became independent thanks to a special statute of 1579.*
According to tradition, spaghetti *were the main pastas used to prepare a dish with* pesce fuggito *("escaped fish"): Sometimes, in the absence of anything better, real fish was replaced with ingredients such as seaweed or porous rocks from the seabed, which, boiled with various spices, created a savory fish-flavored broth in which to cook the pasta. These special recipes also inspired the famous* acqua pazza *("crazy water") from Lazio.*

《*In Amalfi, the sea was our food. As kids first and as youngsters later, we fed on the sea. At the beach, we would dip a tarallo into the brine. When wet, it became soft and tasty. We would wait for the wave and just reach out our hand. [...]*
Later, in the dark, to avoid being seen, the women would come to fill their small earthenware jars. They would step into the water barefoot, twining their skirts above their knees and dipping their jars, which would fill with a quick gurgle. Every now and then someone would be fined: it was forbidden by law to take water from the sea. But, in the end, the officer would give in to the pleadings and the signs of respect, and would revoke the fine. What was important was to never be without seawater at home.
Cooking spaghetti by mixing a cup of saltwater to freshwater meant giving them such bite that they, seasoned with garlic and olive oil, tomato, parsley, and chili pepper, not only remained 'al dente,' to the point of making a noise if a single strand fell into the dish, but they also acquired the taste of fish. As a matter of fact, the real name of this soup is spaghetti with fujuto fish—in other words, the 'fish that got away.' A pearl of peasant cooking.》
From: Afeltra, Gaetano, *Spaghetti all'acqua di mare*, Salerno (I), Avagliano, 1996, pp. 60-64.

LONG DURUM WHEAT PASTA
Average size *spaghetti*:
length 255.00 mm • diameter 1.67 mm
Average size *spaghettini*:
length 255.00 mm • diameter 1.42 mm

NEAPOLITAN REGINETTE

DRY, WITH HARE OR RABBIT,
GAME AND CHEESES.

Tuscany, and as an industrial product, all regions of Italy.

The wavy edges of this pasta are considered reminiscent of the scalloped edges of crowns worn by princesses and queens, hence the name *reginette*, or "little queens." It is also known by the names of *fettuccelle ricce*, *lasagnette*, *nastrini*, *sciabò* (from the French term jabot, the frills or ruffles decorating the front of a shirt, below the collar), or *signorine* ("young ladies"), referring to the lace typical of female clothing.

Belonging to the family of tagliatelle ricce, *that is, those pastas obtained from a sheet of dough and cut with a toothed pasta cutter,* reginette *were dedicated to Princess Mafalda of Savoy, daughter of Victor Emmanuel III, in Naples in 1902, and their name was changed to* mafaldine. *The marked curls along the edges, reminiscent of the precious lace of a sophisticated dress, are ideal with tomato-based sauces thickened with ricotta and Parmigiano Reggiano cheese. Topped with a basil leaf, they create a patriotic dish flaunting the Italian national colors.*
In 1911 they were also dubbed tripolini, *with reference to the war*

in Libya, and in particular the Libyan city of Tripoli and the architectural style of its buildings.

Girolamo Aleandri in *La difesa dell'Adone* (Venice 1630), on depicting a scene from life at court, makes an unusual mention of long pasta: ≪*A few gentlemen were at play... when one of them said to the others, in jest, that he was drunk on tagliatelle, that is, those strips of dough that in many places in Lombardy are known as lasagnette.*≫
From: Mondelli, Mariaelena, *Antico e vero come la pasta. Ricerca ragionata delle fonti storiche e documentali*, Parma (I), 1998, p. 24.

LONG, FLAT DURUM WHEAT PASTA
Average size:
length 245.00 mm • width 12.20 mm • central thickness 1.18 mm

VERMICELLI / VERMICELLINI

DRY WITH FISH SAUCE,
OR BROKEN UP IN BROTH.

Southern Italy.

Ancient dictionaries define *vermicelli* as "strings of pasta in the likeness of long worms." It is curious that today, Italians generally feel repugnance or disgust at the thought of *vermi* (worms), and yet this does not occur at the mention of the long pasta known as *vermicelli*. Vermicelli are often taken for *spaghetti* or, when fine, for *capelli d'angelo* and *spaghettini*.

Often considered the twin of spaghetti, this type of pasta is distinguished and defined by size as vermicelli, vermicellini, vermicelloni, capellini, capelli d'angelo, *and so on.*
This is one of the oldest pasta varieties, first mentioned in 1475 by Bartolomeo Platina, originally named Sacchi, in his Latin De honesta voluptate. In the chapter In vermiculos, *he speaks of* vermicelli *made "ad latitudinem unius diguli," that is, as big as our cannelloni; on fasting days, they were cooked in lightly salted boiling water rather than a fatty stock, and were seasoned, according to the Renaissance fashion, with cheese, butter, sugar, and sweet spices.*

Today, vermicelli *are particularly widespread in southern Italy, where they are generally cooked with seafood.*

≪*We crossed the main road in Gragnano, strewn with macaroni as far as the eye could see. On the sides of the roads, macaroni of every shape and size hung from high fences or were laid out on cloths. Some, called vermicelli, were thin like twine, while others, referred to as ziti, had the circumference of a pipe. If, indeed, macaroni are to the Neapolitans what roast beef is to the English, in Gragnano, this inexhaustible availability of their favorite food would make their heart burst with joy.*≫
From: Mancusi Sorrentino, Lejla, *Maccheronea. Storia, aneddoti, proverbi, letteratura e tante ricette*, Naples (I), Grimaldi & C., 2000, pp. 131-132.

LONG DURUM WHEAT PASTA
Average size *vermicelli*:
length 255.00 mm • diameter 2.07 mm
Average size *vermicellini*:
length 255.00 mm • diameter 1.89 mm

NEAPOLITAN ZITI

Southern Italy, in particular Sicily, and now widespread in all regions of Italy.

The name comes from the Sicilian term *zita*, meaning "bride-to-be," as this pasta was once de rigueur at weddings. In standard Italian, the only form of this term to survive is *zitella*, meaning "spinster."

This is a pasta for feast days in different regions of southern Italy, such as Molise, Puglia, and Sicily. Popular belief in Molise, for example, called for making it on the Feast of the Epiphany (January 6) to ward off seeing the devil on one's deathbed. In Sicily, it is connected with weddings, as the term zita still means "bride-to-be" today. On these occasions, it was traditional to bring a gift of a hearty plate of pasta to all the neighbors, who were generously invited to share in the family celebrations. In Puglia, zite were used for pasta seduta, or "seated pasta": the pasta was covered with tomato sauce, meatballs, and grated cheese, then poured into a bowl, where it remained "seated" for some minutes, while the covered bowl was immersed in a boiling bain-marie.

《*It was a Sunday. In our house, the stewed zitoni were already ready, as was customary in Naples in those days of plenty: large macaroni, first wrapped in a rich and velvety meat sauce and then cooked in the oven. And yet, no one had taken a bite, despite filling the air with their delightful scent, because Uncle Raffaele was sick, delirious, burning up [with fever], and everyone feared the worst. In the middle of the night, Uncle Raffaele rose from the bed in his long nightshirt, went barefoot into the kitchen, put his hands into the pot brimming with stewed ziti, and began to devour them: he had eaten half the contents of the pot when granddad, awakened by the bustle, rushed to pull him away from this deadly deed and aroused the entire household to warn them of the imminent disaster. Except that the disaster never actually happened: we children, gathered around Uncle Raffaele's bed, instead of witnessing his passing due to indigestion, watched on as he slept blissfully, his fever put to flight by that epic feed on stewed zitoni, which, more than any medicine, restored Uncle Raffaele's body to health.*》·
From: Stefanile, Mario, *Invito ai Maccheroni*, Naples (I), Montanino, [1950], pp. 29-39.

LONG, HOLLOW DURUM WHEAT PASTA
Average size:
length 245.00 mm • diameter 7.80 mm • thickness 1.10 mm

BAVETTE AL CARTOCCIO WITH SEAFOOD AND CRISPY VEGETABLES

PREPARATION: 40 minutes
COOKING TIME: 40 minutes
DIFFICULTY: HIGH

4 SERVINGS

12 oz. (350 g) Barilla bavette
2 3/4 oz. (80 g) jumbo shrimp, shelled and deveined
10 1/2 oz. (300 g) mussels
3 1/2 oz. (100 g) small squid
5 oz. (150 g) scorpion fish, striped bass, or red snapper, filleted
3 1/2 oz. (100 g) baby octopus
11 oz. (300 g) clams, preferably carpet shell clams, if available
2 tbsp. (40 ml) extra-virgin olive oil, plus more for drizzling
1 3/4 oz. (50 g) zucchini, or about 1/4 medium
1 3/4 oz. (50 g) carrot, or about 1 small
1 oz. (30 g) celery, or about 1 stalk
1 1/2 oz. (40 g) eggplant
3 1/2 oz. (100 g) sweet cherry tomatoes, such as Datterini
1 bunch parsley, chopped
1 bunch basil
3 cloves garlic
Crushed red chile pepper to taste
Salt to taste

ALTERNATIVE VERSIONS

For this recipe, you can use other long pasta, such as spaghetti, instead of bavette.

Bring a pot of salted water to a boil for the bavette. Meanwhile, thoroughly soak and clean the clams and the mussels (and debeard the mussels), rinsing well to remove all sand and grit. In two separate pans, heat 1 tablespoon of olive oil in each and sauté garlic and parsley stems. Add the mussels in one pan and the clams in the other, and cook until they are fully open (discarding any that do not open). Remove some of the shells, filter the juices (discarding the garlic and parsley stems), and place the mollusks in a bowl with the filtered juices.

Clean, wash, and julienne all the vegetables, then quickly sauté them in a pan with a drizzle of olive oil. Thoroughly clean the squid, then cut it into strips. Repeat with the baby octopus.

Skin, bone, and dice the scorpion fish (or bass or snapper). In a frying pan, quickly sear scorpion fish (or bass or snapper), and then sear the shrimp. Toss the tomatoes quickly in a pan over medium-high heat and season with salt (the tomatoes should be lightly browned but remain intact).

Cook the bavette in the pot of boiling salted water for half the time indicated for al dente; drain. Meanwhile, in a large skillet, combine all the previously prepared ingredients with half the filtered juices. Toss the pasta with the sauce, mixing well. Season with salt and crushed chile pepper.

Heat the oven to 350°F (175°C). Cut 4 sheets of parchment paper or aluminum foil and divide the bavette evenly on top of each. Drizzle with olive oil, scatter with a few basil leaves and some parsley, and fold the sheets into parcels. Bake for about 10 minutes and serve.

BAVETTE
WITH PESTO AND CLAMS

PREPARATION: 30 minutes
COOKING TIME: 15 minutes
DIFFICULTY: EASY

4 SERVINGS

12 oz. (350 g) Barilla bavette
2 1/4 lb. (1 kg) clams
1 oz. (30 g) fresh basil
1/2 oz. (15 g) pine nuts
2 oz. (60 g) Parmigiano Reggiano
cheese, grated
1 1/2 oz. (40 g) aged Pecorino
cheese, grated
3 1/2 oz. (100 g) green
beans, chopped
7 oz. (200 g) potatoes,
peeled and diced
7 oz. (200 ml) extra-virgin olive oil
(preferably from Liguria)
1 clove garlic
Salt

Soak the clams in cold water to release any grit; scrub under running water. Put the clams in a covered skillet (with no additional liquid) over high heat until they open. Discard any clams that do not open. Remove the pan from heat, discard the top shells, and filter the cooking juices, returning them to the pan.

Rinse and dry the basil. Using a mortar and pestle (or pulsing in a blender), grind the basil, pine nuts, and whole garlic clove with 5 ounces (150 ml) of olive oil, a pinch of salt, and the grated cheeses. Pour the mixture into a bowl and cover with the remaining oil.

Bring a pot of salted water to a boil. Cook the potatoes and the green beans together with the bavette until the pasta is al dente. Drain, reserving a little of the cooking water. Toss pasta for a few minutes in the pan with the clams and their juices. Remove the pan from heat, season the pasta with the pesto, and mix well, diluting the sauce with a little of the pasta water and a drizzle of olive oil.

ALTERNATIVE VERSIONS
This tasty pesto and clam sauce is ideal with long semolina pasta, such as spaghetti, spaghettini, and vermicelli.

BAVETTE WITH JUMBO SHRIMP

PREPARATION: 20 minutes
COOKING TIME: 20 minutes
DIFFICULTY: **MEDIUM**

4 SERVINGS

12 oz. (350 g) Barilla bavette
12 jumbo shrimp
7 oz. (200 g) cherry
tomatoes, quartered
2 tbsp. (30 ml) white wine
1/4 cup (60 ml) extra-virgin olive oil
1 oz. (30 g) fresh parsley, chopped
1 red chile pepper,
seeded and chopped
1 clove garlic
Salt to taste

Clean, shell, and devein the shrimp. Cut them in half lengthwise.

Heat 2 tablespoons of oil in pan and sauté the whole garlic clove. Before it begins to brown, add the chile pepper and the shrimp. Sear them quickly and pour in the white wine. Cook until the wine evaporates. Add the tomatoes and cook for 5 minutes, seasoning with salt and parsley.

Meanwhile, bring a pot of salted water to a boil and cook the bavette until it is al dente. Drain, reserving some of the cooking water. Transfer pasta to the pan with the shrimp sauce and toss together. Sauté, adding a few tablespoons of pasta water and the remaining 2 tablespoons of oil.

ALTERNATIVE VERSIONS
For this recipe you can also use other long pastas, such as spaghetti, vermicelli, and spaghetti alla chitarra.

BAVETTE WITH CLAMS

PREPARATION: 20 minutes
COOKING TIME: 15 minutes
DIFFICULTY: EASY

4 SERVINGS

12 oz. (350 g) Barilla bavette
2 1/4 lb. (1 kg) clams
1/2 cup (100 ml) extra-virgin olive oil
1 tbsp. chopped parsley
1 clove garlic, crushed
Salt and pepper to taste

Bring a large pot of salted water to a boil for the pasta.

Scrub and rinse the clams thoroughly under running water. Place them in a large skillet with 1 tablespoon of oil over medium heat. Cover with a lid and cook them until they open (2 to 3 minutes), discarding any clams that do not open. Remove the skillet from heat and shell half of the clams. Strain the cooking liquid and pour it back into the skillet with the clams for the sauce. Set aside.

In another skillet, sauté the garlic in the remaining oil until golden brown. Add the clams and the sauce and cook until it comes to a boil.

Meanwhile, cook the bavette in the boiling salted water until al dente. Drain, reserving some of the cooking water. Toss the bavette with clams and sauce, adding cooking water as needed. Sprinkle generously with pepper and chopped parsley.

ALTERNATIVE VERSIONS
This recipe is best with long pasta. The bavette can be substituted with spaghetti or vermicellini.

I ♥ Pasta

WHOLE-GRAIN BAVETTE WITH SHRIMP, FENNEL, AND FISH ROE

PREPARATION: 20 minutes

COOKING TIME: 8 minutes

DIFFICULTY: EASY

4 SERVINGS

12 oz. (350 g) Barilla whole-grain bavette
16 jumbo shrimp
1 medium fennel bulb
7 oz. (200 g) cherry tomatoes, halved
1/2 cup (100 ml) heavy cream
2 3/4 tbsp. (40 ml) extra-virgin olive oil
1 oz. (30 g) fish roe
Salt and pepper to taste

Clean and devein the shrimp, remove the heads and shells (leaving tail sections attached), and sauté them in a pan with half the oil. Set aside.

Bring a pot of salted water to a boil for the bavette.

Julienne the fennel bulb, setting aside the fronds for a garnish. Sauté julienned fennel in the same pan used for the shrimp, with the remaining oil. Season with salt and pepper, and cook for 2 to 3 minutes.

Add the heavy cream and the cherry tomatoes to the fennel, and continue cooking for about 5 minutes. One minute before removing the pan from heat, add the shrimp and allow them to warm through.

Cook the bavette in the boiling salted water until it is al dente; drain. Toss together with the sauce. Before serving, sprinkle the pasta with grated or flaked roe and garnish with the fennel fronds.

ALTERNATIVE VERSIONS

Other long pastas are also excellent with this recipe, such as regular (non-whole-grain) bavette and spaghetti.

BUCATINI AMATRICIANA

PREPARATION: 15 minutes
COOKING TIME: 10 minutes
DIFFICULTY: EASY

4 SERVINGS

9 oz. (250 g) Barilla bucatini
5 oz. (150 g) pork jowl
(guanciale) or bacon
3 1/2 oz. (100 g) onion, peeled and
thinly sliced
4 ripe tomatoes
1/2 cup (40 g) grated
Pecorino Romano cheese
1/4 cup (50 ml) extra-virgin olive oil
Crushed red chile pepper to taste
Salt and black pepper to taste

Bring a large pot of salted water to a boil for the bucatini.

Meanwhile, cut the guanciale or bacon into slices and then into rectangles. Add it to a pan over medium heat, along with a very small amount of water. Simmer meat so that the fat melts.

Prepare the tomatoes by making an X-shaped incision on the bottom of each tomato and blanching it in boiling water for 10 to 15 seconds. Immediately dip the tomatoes in ice water, then peel them, remove the seeds and dice them.

Remove the guanciale or bacon pieces from the pan and drain them thoroughly. Add the oil to the pan and sauté the onions. Add the tomatoes. Season with the crushed red chile pepper, salt, and black pepper. Return the guanciale or bacon pieces to the pan with the tomato sauce and heat briefly.

Cook the bucatini in the pot of boiling salted water until al dente; drain. Toss pasta with the sauce, sprinkle with the Pecorino Romano, and serve hot.

ALTERNATIVE VERSIONS
In addition to bucatini, this classic recipe from Lazio is excellent with spaghetti and spaghetti alla chitarra.

I ♥ Pasta

CAPELLINI WITH SAUSAGE AND SAFFRON

PREPARATION: 30 minutes
COOKING TIME: 25 minutes
DIFFICULTY: MEDIUM

4 SERVINGS

12 oz. (350 g) Barilla capellini
11 oz. (300 g) sausage
5 oz. (150 g) leeks
2/3 cup (150 ml) heavy cream
1/4 cup (60 ml) extra-virgin olive oil
Pinch of (0.5 g) saffron
Salt and pepper to taste

Clean and finely slice only the white parts of the leeks. Heat 2 tablespoons of oil in a pan over low heat and sauté the leeks until softened.

Remove sausage casing and crumble the sausage. Heat the remaining 2 tablespoons of oil in a skillet over medium heat and sauté the sausage. When the sausage is well browned, discard the melted fat and add the sausage to the leeks. Continue cooking for 5 minutes, adding a little water if the sauce begins to dry out. Add the heavy cream and saffron and simmer very gently.

Meanwhile, bring a pot of salted water to a boil and cook the capellini until it is al dente; drain. Transfer pasta to the pan with the sauce and stir over medium heat for a few minutes to combine.

ALTERNATIVE VERSIONS
This sauce is perfect with long semolina pastas such as spaghettini and spaghetti, or with egg pasta such as fettuccine.

I ♥ Pasta

LASAGNETTE / LONG PASTA

LASAGNETTE WITH EGGPLANT AND BEEF-AND-VEAL RAGÙ

PREPARATION: 50 minutes

COOKING TIME: 1 hour

DIFFICULTY: MEDIUM

4 SERVINGS

12 oz. (350 g) Barilla lasagnette
7 oz. (200 g) ground beef
3 1/2 oz. (100 g) ground veal
1/2 tbsp. (20 g) butter
3/4 oz. (20 g) ricotta
2/3 cup (60 g) grated
Parmigiano Reggiano cheese
1 lb. 5 oz. (600 g) tomatoes, chopped
1 3/4 oz. (50 g) prosciutto, chopped
1/2 cup (100 ml) dry white wine
¼ cup (50 ml) extra-virgin olive oil
1/2 onion, peeled and sliced
1 eggplant
Salt and pepper to taste

Peel and cut the eggplant into 1/2-inch (1-2 cm) dice, then put it in a colander, salt it lightly and allow it to drain for about 30 minutes.

Heat 2 tablespoons of oil and all the butter in a skillet over medium. Sauté the prosciutto and the onion, then add the ground meat. Raise the heat to medium-high and brown the meat and onion, then add the wine, cooking until the wine evaporates completely. Add the tomatoes and enough water to cover the meat. Season with salt and pepper and bring to a boil. Reduce heat to medium, cover the pan, and continue cooking for about 40 minutes.

Toss eggplant in a pan with the remaining 2 tablespoons of oil. Add the meat ragù a few minutes before eggplant is fully cooked.

Meanwhile, bring a large pot of salted water to a boil and cook the lasagnette until it is al dente; drain. Toss pasta to combine with the meat-and-eggplant ragù and the grated Parmigiano Reggiano.

ALTERNATIVE VERSIONS

This recipe is also excellent with other long pastas, such as egg tagliatelle, spaghetti alla chitarra, spaghettoni, and bucatini.

I ♥ Pasta

LASAGNETTE
WITH LAMB AND ARTICHOKE RAGÙ

PREPARATION: 30 minutes
COOKING TIME: 25 minutes
DIFFICULTY: EASY

4 SERVINGS

12 oz. (350 g) Barilla
semolina lasagnette
11 oz. (300 g) lean lamb, diced
4 artichokes
1/4 cup (60 ml) extra-virgin olive oil
1/2 cup (100 ml) dry white wine
3 1/2 oz. (100 g) tomatoes, peeled
and chopped
1/2 cup (100 ml) beef broth,
as needed
1 cup (80 g) shaved
Pecorino cheese
1 sprig rosemary
1 sprig thyme
1 fresh bay leaf
1 clove garlic
1 onion, peeled and chopped
Juice of 1 lemon
Salt and pepper to taste

ALTERNATIVE VERSIONS
This recipe also goes well with
egg pasta, such as pappardelle,
fettuccine ricce, and spaghetti
alla chitarra.

Clean artichokes by slicing at least 1/4 inch (1/2 cm) off the tops and bottoms and removing all the tough outer leaves. Cut the artichokes in half lengthwise and remove the chokes. Cut into thin slices and soak in a bowl of water with the lemon juice to prevent the artichokes from turning black.

In a skillet, heat 2 tablespoons of oil and brown the chopped onion with the whole garlic clove, the bay leaf, and the whole rosemary and thyme. Add the lamb and allow it to brown. Season with salt and pepper, then add the white wine. Let the wine evaporate completely, then add the chopped tomatoes and let the mixture simmer for about 15 minutes, adding some broth, if necessary.

Meanwhile, sauté the artichokes with the remaining 2 tablespoons of oil and season with a sprinkling of salt. Add the artichokes to the lamb and continue cooking for another 5 minutes.

Bring a pot of salted water to a boil and cook the lasagnette until it is al dente; drain. Toss pasta with the sauce, sprinkle with shaved Pecorino, and serve.

I ♥ Pasta

MACCHERONCINI WITH RADICCHIO, WALNUTS, AND TALEGGIO CREAM

PREPARATION: 30 minutes
COOKING TIME: 20 minutes
DIFFICULTY: MEDIUM

4 SERVINGS

12 oz. (350 g) Barilla maccheroncini
3 1/2 oz. (100 g) radicchio, finely chopped
10 walnuts, peeled
3 1/2 oz. (100 g) Taleggio cheese
1/4 cup (50 ml) heavy cream
1/3 cup (30 g) grated Parmigiano Reggiano cheese
3/4 oz. (20 g) white onion, peeled and minced
2 tsp. (10 ml) extra-virgin olive oil
4 fresh basil leaves
Salt and pepper to taste

Bring a pot of salted water to a boil for the maccheroncini.

Meanwhile, heat the olive oil in a large pan and sauté the minced onion for 3 to 4 minutes. Add the radicchio, season with salt and pepper, and cook for a few more minutes.

Melt the Taleggio in a saucepan with the heavy cream. When the mixture has melted, add the grated Parmigiano Reggiano and season with salt. For a smoother cream, blend the mixture in a blender and keep it warm.

Cook the maccheroncini in the pot of boiling salted water until it is just al dente; drain. Transfer pasta to the pan with the radicchio, add the walnuts and the whole basil leaves, and stir to combine. Pour the hot Taleggio cream on a serving dish and arrange the pasta on top. Serve immediately.

ALTERNATIVE VERSIONS
Other pastas are also excellent with this dish, such as egg pappardelle, pennette rigate, and mezze maniche rigate.

NEAPOLITAN REGINETTE WITH NEAPOLITAN RAGÙ

PREPARATION: 2 1/2 hours
COOKING TIME: 25 minutes
DIFFICULTY: EASY

4 SERVINGS

12 oz. (350 g) Barilla Neapolitan reginette
1/2 cup (100 ml) extra-virgin olive oil
7 oz. (200 g) yellow onions, peeled and chopped
2 pork ribs, 2 1/2 oz. (75 g) each
7 oz. (200 g) lean beef
7 oz. (200 g) beef shank
2/3 cup (150 ml) red wine
2 1/4 lb. (1 kg) tomato sauce
6 fresh basil leaves
Salt and pepper to taste

Cut the lean beef and beef shank into serving pieces. Heat the oil in a large pot over medium and add the onions, basil, pork ribs, lean beef, and beef shank, then add the red wine. Cook until the wine has evaporated completely, then add the tomato sauce and cook for at least 2 hours, stirring occasionally.

Season with salt and pepper.

Bring a pot of salted water to a boil and cook the Neapolitan reginette until it is al dente; drain. Remove the meat from the sauce and keep warm. Toss the pasta with the sauce and serve. Serve the meat as a second course.

ALTERNATIVE VERSIONS
Neapolitan ragù is excellent with other pastas, such as Neapolitan ziti, penne a candela, and fusilli.

I ♥ Pasta

SPAGHETTI CARBONARA

PREPARATION: **10 minutes**

COOKING TIME: **8 minutes**

DIFFICULTY: **EASY**

4 SERVINGS

12 oz. (350 g) spaghetti
5 1/3 oz. (150 g) pork jowl
(guanciale) or bacon
4 large egg yolks
3 1/2 oz. (100 g) Pecorino Romano
cheese, grated, or about
1/3 cup plus 1 tbsp.
Salt and pepper to taste

Bring a large pot of salted water to a boil for the spaghetti.

Beat the egg yolks in a bowl with a pinch of salt and a little Pecorino Romano. Cut the guanciale or bacon into thin strips, about 1/12 inches (2 mm) thick, or into a small dice. Sauté the guanciale in a large saucepan over medium heat.

Cook the spaghetti in the boiling salted water until al dente. Drain, reserving some of the cooking water. Transfer the spaghetti to the skillet with the guanciale or bacon and toss together. Remove from the heat and add the egg yolk mixture and a little cooking water, and mix for about 30 seconds. Mix in the remaining Pecorino and a dash of pepper, and serve immediately.

ALTERNATIVE VERSIONS
This traditional Roman dish can also be prepared with other long pasta, such as spaghetti alla chitarra and vermicelli.

SPAGHETTI IN TOMATO SAUCE

PREPARATION: 30 minutes
COOKING TIME: 25 minutes
DIFFICULTY: EASY

4 SERVINGS

12 oz. (350 g) Barilla spaghetti
2 tbsp. (30 ml) extra-virgin olive oil
1 3/4 lb. (600 g) tomatoes, peeled and chopped
3 1/2 oz. (100 g) onion, peeled and chopped
1/3 cup plus 1 ½ tbsp. (40 g) grated Parmigiano Reggiano cheese
8 fresh basil leaves
1 clove garlic
1 tsp. sugar (4 g) (optional)
Salt and pepper to taste

Heat the oil in a frying pan over medium and sauté the onion and whole garlic clove until golden brown. Add the tomatoes and season with salt and pepper. Raise heat to high and cook for about 20 minutes, stirring occasionally.

Meanwhile, bring a large pot of salted water to a boil for the spaghetti.

Remove the garlic clove and add the basil to the onion-tomato mixture. If the tomatoes are particularly acidic, you can add a teaspoon of sugar.

Cook the spaghetti in the boiling salted water until al dente; drain. Toss the pasta with the sauce and top with Parmigiano Reggiano.

ALTERNATIVE VERSIONS
The sauce is suitable for both long and short pasta shapes. The pastas that enhance the sauce most are: penne rigate, penne lisce, farfalle, fusilli, bavette, spaghettini, and, for egg pasta, tagliatelle.

I ❤ Pasta

SPAGHETTI WITH CLAMS

PREPARATION: 15 minutes
COOKING TIME: 8 minutes
DIFFICULTY: EASY

4 SERVINGS

12 1/2 oz. (350 g) Barilla spaghetti
1/4 cup (50 ml) extra-virgin olive oil
10 1/2 oz. (300 g) clams
10 1/2 oz. (300 g) ripe tomatoes
Approx. 1/2 cup (100 ml) white wine
1 clove garlic
1 sprig parsley, chopped
Crushed red chile pepper
flakes to taste
Salt to taste

Bring a large pot of salted water to a boil for the spaghetti. Scrub and rinse the clams thoroughly under running water. Place them in a large skillet over medium heat with 2 tablespoons of oil, the whole garlic clove, the chopped parsley, the white wine, and crushed red chile pepper flakes. Cover and cook until the clams open (2 to 3 minutes), discarding any clams that do not open. Remove the skillet from the heat and remove the shells. Strain the cooking liquid and set juices and clams aside.

Prepare the tomatoes by making an X-shaped incision on the bottom of each tomato and blanching it in boiling water for 10 to 15 seconds. Immediately dip the tomatoes in ice water, then peel and seed them and cut them into strips. In another pan, heat the remaining 2 tablespoons of oil and add the tomatoes. Season with salt and cook for a couple of minutes. Add the clams and the filtered juices and simmer.

Meanwhile, cook the spaghetti in the boiling salted water until al dente; drain, reserving some of the cooking water. Toss pasta in the pan with the clam sauce, adding cooking water as needed.

ALTERNATIVE VERSIONS
This seafood sauce is ideal with long pastas, such as bavette, vermicelli, and spaghettini.

SPAGHETTI WITH MARINATED TOMATO AND HARD RICOTTA

PREPARATION: 10 minutes
RESTING TIME: 2-3 hours
COOKING TIME: 8 minutes
DIFFICULTY: EASY

4 SERVINGS

12 oz. (350 g) Barilla spaghetti
1 lb. 2 oz. (500 g)
beefsteak tomatoes
2 oz. (60 g) hard ricotta
(ricotta salata)
1/4 cup (50 ml) extra-virgin
olive oil
10 fresh basil leaves, rinsed, dried,
and hand-torn
1 clove garlic, finely chopped
Salt and pepper to taste

Rinse, halve, and seed the tomatoes, then thinly slice them. Place them in a large salad bowl with the oil, basil, and garlic and season with salt and pepper. Stir to combine. Let the tomato mixture marinate at room temperature for 2 to 3 hours.

Bring a pot of salted water to a boil and cook the spaghetti until it is al dente; drain. Transfer spaghetti to the bowl with the tomato mixture and toss to combine.

Grate the hard ricotta and sprinkle it over spaghetti before serving.

ALTERNATIVE VERSIONS
As this sauce is excellent with both long and short pasta, you can choose other shapes such as vermicelli, bavette, rigatoni, and orecchiette pugliesi.

SPAGHETTINI WITH GARLIC, OIL, AND CHILE PEPPER

PREPARATION: 10 minutes
COOKING TIME: 5 minutes
DIFFICULTY: EASY

4 SERVINGS

12 oz. (350 g) Barilla spaghettini
1/3 cup (70 ml) extra-virgin olive oil
1 tsp. chopped fresh parsley
1 clove garlic, sliced
1 fresh chile pepper,
seeded and sliced
Salt to taste

Bring a pot of salted water to a boil for the spaghettini and cook until it is al dente. Drain pasta, reserving some cooking water.

Heat the oil in a medium skillet over medium heat. Lightly sauté the garlic, and, after a few moments, add the parsley and the chile pepper, preventing the ingredients from browning by adding a small ladle of pasta water.

Toss pasta in the pan with the sauce, mixing well. Serve hot.

ALTERNATIVE VERSIONS
This simple yet extremely tasty sauce is ideal with long pasta, preferably made from semolina, such as spaghetti, vermicelli, and bavette.

I ♥ Pasta

SPAGHETTINI WITH HAKE AND FRESH OREGANO

PREPARATION: 30 minutes
COOKING TIME: 20 minutes
DIFFICULTY: MEDIUM

4 SERVINGS

12 oz. (350 g) Barilla spaghettini
1 lb. 2 oz. (500 g) hake, cleaned, filleted, and chopped
7 oz. (200 g) cherry tomatoes, quartered
1/4 cup extra-virgin olive oil
1 sprig oregano
Zest of 1 lemon, grated
1 clove garlic, minced
Salt and freshly ground black pepper to taste

Bring a pot of salted water to a boil for the pasta.

Heat the olive oil in a pan over medium and sauté the garlic until it is golden. Add the tomatoes and the oregano leaves and cook for 10 minutes.

Add the hake and season lightly with salt and pepper. Add the grated lemon zest, and cook for 4 to 5 minutes.

Cook the spaghettini in the pot of boiling salted water until it is al dente; drain. Toss pasta with the sauce, a couple dashes of black pepper, and serve.

ALTERNATIVE VERSIONS
This recipe is also excellent with other pastas, either short, such as trofie, or long, such as vermicelli and bavette.

VERMICELLI WITH PUTTANESCA SAUCE

PREPARATION: 30 minutes
COOKING TIME: 13 minutes
DIFFICULTY: EASY

4 SERVINGS

12 oz. (350 g) Barilla vermicelli
1 lb. 2 oz. (500 g) tomatoes, peeled and chopped
1 3/4 oz. (50 g) black olives, pitted and halved or sliced
1 oz. (30 g) salted capers, rinsed and coarsely chopped
2 tbsp. (30 ml) extra-virgin olive oil
1 oz. (30 g) anchovy fillets in oil
1-2 cloves garlic
3/4 oz. (20 g) fresh parsley, chopped
Red chile pepper, fresh or dried, to taste
Salt to taste

Bring a pot of salted water to a boil for the vermicelli.

Thinly slice either 1 or 2 whole garlic cloves, as you prefer. In a large skillet, cook the garlic in olive oil until golden brown, adding some chile pepper to taste. (If you are using a fresh chile, seed and slice it; dry chile can be crumbled by hand, using disposable gloves.)

Add the capers to the browned garlic and chile, together with the anchovy fillets. Continue cooking over low heat for 2 minutes.

Raise the heat to high and add the tomatoes. Season with salt, if needed, and continue cooking over high heat for about 5 minutes, stirring occasionally. Add the olives to the sauce.

Cook the vermicelli in the boiling salted water until it is al dente; drain. Toss the pasta with the sauce, sprinkle with the chopped parsley, and serve.

ALTERNATIVE VERSIONS
This traditional Neapolitan dish is ideal with long pastas, such as spaghetti, bavette, and spaghettini.

VERMICELLI WITH MUSSELS

PREPARATION: 1 hour
COOKING TIME: 13 minutes
DIFFICULTY: MEDIUM

4 SERVINGS

12 oz. (350 g) Barilla vermicelli
18 oz. (500 g) peeled
tomatoes, minced
1 3/4 lb. (800 g) mussels
1/4 cup (60 ml) extra-virgin olive oil
1/3 cup (20 g) fresh
parsley, chopped
4-5 fresh basil leaves
1 clove garlic
Crushed red chile pepper
flakes to taste
Salt and pepper to taste

Heat the olive oil in a skillet and lightly fry the whole, peeled garlic clove, the red chile pepper flakes, and parsley.

Thoroughly soak, clean, and debeard the mussels, rinsing well to remove all sand and grit. Add them to the pan and cook until they have opened (discard any mussels that have not opened). Filter the cooking juices and discard the shells.

Add the tomatoes to the mussels and their juices, season with salt and pepper, and cook for a couple of minutes, then keep warm.

Bring a pot of salted water to a boil and cook the vermicelli until it is al dente; drain. Transfer pasta to the pan with the mussels and sauce, along with the basil, and toss to combine.

ALTERNATIVE VERSIONS
This classic mussel sauce is also excellent with spaghetti, bavette, or lasagnette.

I ♥ Pasta

VERMICELLINI IN SQUID INK SAUCE

PREPARATION: 10 minutes
COOKING TIME: 11 minutes
DIFFICULTY: EASY

4 SERVINGS

12 oz. (350 g) Barilla vermicellini
14 oz. (400 g) tomatoes,
preferably San Marzano, diced
1/2 oz. (15 g) squid ink
2 tbsp. plus 1 tsp. (35 ml)
extra-virgin olive oil
1 oz. (30 g) fresh parsley, chopped
1 clove garlic
1 red chile pepper, seeded
and chopped
Salt to taste

Wash, seed, and dice the tomatoes.

Bring a pot of salted water to a boil and cook the vermicellini until it is al dente; drain, reserving some of the pasta water.

Meanwhile, heat the oil in a skillet with the whole garlic clove, then add the parsley (setting a little aside as garnish) and the chile pepper. Sauté for 1 minute and then add the tomatoes. Cook for another minute, then add the squid ink and dilute with a small ladle of the pasta water. Let the liquid reduce slightly over low heat for 2 to 3 minutes, then season with salt.

Toss the pasta with the sauce, sprinkle with minced parsley, and serve.

ALTERNATIVE VERSIONS
This recipe is best paired with long semolina or egg pasta. Instead of vermicelli, you can use spaghettini and spaghetti, or, as egg pasta, tagliolini and spaghetti alla chitarra.

NEAPOLITAN ZITI WITH FRIED EGGPLANT AND MEATBALLS

PREPARATION: 1 hour
COOKING TIME: 25 minutes
OVEN COOKING TIME: 5-6 minutes
DIFFICULTY: MEDIUM

4 SERVINGS

12 oz. (350 g) Barilla Neapolitan ziti
1 lb. (450 g) tomatoes, chopped
11 oz. (300 g) eggplant
5 oz. (150 g) ground beef
1/4 cup (50 ml) milk
1 cup (80 g) grated
Parmigiano Reggiano cheese
¼ cup (30 g) all-purpose flour
1 3/4 oz. (50 g) onion, peeled
and chopped
1 3/4 oz. (50 g) carrot, chopped
1 3/4 oz. (50 g) celery, chopped
1/4 cup (50 ml) extra-virgin olive
oil, plus more for drizzling
1/3 cup (30 g) breadcrumbs
1 bread roll
5-6 fresh basil leaves,
roughly chopped
1 tbsp. chopped parsley
1 clove garlic, crushed
Vegetable oil for frying, as needed
Salt and pepper to taste

ALTERNATIVE VERSIONS
This recipe is also great with tortiglioni, macaroni, and vermicelli.

Peel the eggplant and chop into 1/2-inch (1 cm) cubes. Put it in a colander, salt it lightly, and allow it to drain for about 30 minutes.

Remove and discard the crust from the roll and soak the soft part in the milk. Squeeze out excess milk and chop the bread. In a bowl, mix bread with the ground beef, the chopped parsley and one-third of the Parmigiano Reggiano. Season with salt and pepper.

Shape mixture into small meatballs. Flour them, then brown in a pan with two-thirds of the olive oil.

Heat the remaining olive oil in a pan over medium. Brown the onion, celery, and carrot, along with the garlic. Add the chopped tomatoes, season with salt and pepper, and cook over high heat for about 10 minutes. Add the meatballs.

Heat at least 1/2 inch of vegetable oil in a skillet until hot and shimmering. Fry the diced eggplant, drain with a skimmer, and dry on kitchen paper.

Bring a pot of salted water to a boil for the ziti. With a serrated knife, make two crosswise incisions on each Neapolitan ziti, so that they will break cleanly, and break them into thirds. Cook ziti until it is al dente; drain. In a large bowl, toss with the sauce, the eggplant, and the basil.

If you wish, put the ziti in a greased baking dish, sprinkle with the remaining Parmigiano Reggiano and the breadcrumbs, add a drizzle of olive oil, and bake at 390°F (200°C) for 5 to 6 minutes.

I ♥ Pasta

NEAPOLITAN ZITI AU GRATIN WITH TOMATOES AND BREADCRUMBS

PREPARATION: 30 minutes
COOKING TIME: 15 minutes
DIFFICULTY: EASY

4 SERVINGS

12 oz. (350 g) Barilla Neapolitan ziti
1 3/4 oz. (50 g) onion, peeled and diced
1 3/4 oz. (50 g) carrot, diced
1 3/4 oz. (50 g) celery, diced
1/4 cup (50 ml) extra-virgin olive oil
1 lb. (450 g) tomatoes, peeled and chopped
1 oz. (30 g) dried breadcrumbs
5-6 fresh basil leaves, roughly chopped
1 clove garlic, peeled and crushed
Salt and pepper to taste

Heat the oven to 390°F (200°C).

Heat two-thirds of the oil in a pan over medium and brown onion, celery, carrot, and garlic. Add the chopped tomatoes, season with salt and pepper, and cook over high heat for about 10 minutes.

With a serrated knife, make two crosswise incisions on each Neapolitan ziti, so that they will break cleanly. Break them into thirds.

Bring a pot of salted water to a boil and cook the ziti until al dente; drain. Toss pasta with the sauce and the basil.

Place pasta and sauce in a buttered baking dish, sprinkle with breadcrumbs, drizzle with the remaining oil, and bake in the oven for 5 to 6 minutes.

ALTERNATIVE VERSIONS
This simple-yet-tasty recipe is excellent with other pastas, such as tortiglioni, rigatoni, and pipe rigate.

I ♥ Pasta

SHORT PASTA

AN ODE TO IMAGINATION

Short pasta is an ode to the imagination, undoubtedly offering the greatest variety of shapes, textures, and sizes: from the intertwined "S" shapes of casarecce to the merry farfalle with their serrated wings; from the linear penne, whether smooth or ribbed, to the castellane, inspired by the skirts of Medieval noblewomen; from the hollow spirals of the cellentani to the thinner twirls of fusilli.

Although this considerable variety in short pastas goes hand in hand with an equally great assortment of sauces, it is important, as for any other type of pasta, to choose the right sauce for the right shape. The pairing must be spot-on. Simple, vigorous shapes with a strong personality, such as tortiglioni from Naples and rigatoni from Rome, go particularly well with thick, full-bodied condiments, such as a meat sauce or a fondue with Parmigiano Reggiano cheese and balsamic vinegar, or with rustic flavors, such as a pepper-and-onion sauce. Conversely, pastas as delicate and gentle as pipette rigate—which cocoon the sauce, only to reveal it on the palate—lend themselves to light vegetable or cheese accompaniments, or to a classic fresh tomato-and-basil sauce.

In general, the mini versions of short pastas, attractive especially to children, are great with colorful vegetable accompaniments or creams, such as mini farfalle served with a cauliflower or pumpkin sauce. Whole-grain short pastas, on the other hand, go better with strong sauces—for example, whole-grain pennette rigate with sausage, cabbage, and smoked Provola cheese—than do their white counterparts.

Many short pastas are typical of particular regions of Italy and are suitable for certain accompaniments dictated by local creativity and history: gnocchetti sardi, for example, are ideal with lamb or fish sauces; Ligurian trofie are traditionally paired with a pesto or walnut sauce; and orecchiette, from Puglia, are generally served with turnip greens or fragrant Mediterranean condiments based on olives, cherry tomatoes, and eggplant.

SICILIAN CASARECCE

DRY, WITH SICILIAN PESTO
OR WALNUT SAUCE.

Sicily and southern Italy.

The name stems from the Roman term *casareccio*, meaning a homemade product. This, therefore, is clearly a homemade variety, which came into industrial production only recently.

This typical durum wheat pasta, originally from Sicily, is shaped like a narrow, twisted tube, ideal for absorbing sauce. Traditionally, casarecce are seasoned either with a fresh pesto sauce—ideal for the hot summer months—or with tomato, basil, olive oil, and ricotta cheese, perhaps with a sprinkling of almonds.

Giovan Battista Crisci, in his *Lucerna de Corteggiani*, published in Naples in 1634, cites a long list of pastas known in his day: ≪*Menestre di pasta: Lagenelle di Monache, Maccaroni incavati di Bari. Maccaroni di Palermo, Tagliarini d'ova, Tagliarini di Cagliari, Tagliarini di mollica, Vermicelli siciliani, Vermicelli d'ingegno, Ver-*

micelli d'amito.≫ *Those maccaroni incavati, or "hollow macaroni," are none other than* cavatieddi, *which in 1634 (the same year Crisci's book was published) had already long been exported to Naples and were regularly served at court.*
From: Crisci, Giovan Battista, *Lucerna de Corteggiani ove, in Dialogo si tratta diffusamente delle Corti, così de ventiquattro officii nobili, come de la varietà de cibi per tutto l'anno; e ciascuna Domenica. Et altri banchetti Divisa in sei Capitoli*, Naples (I), Roncaglione, l634, p. 302.

LONG, FLAT DURUM WHEAT PASTA
Average size:
length 50.00 mm • width 5.10 mm • thickness 1.30 mm

CASTELLANE

DRY, WITH CHEESE, VEGETABLE,
OR PUMPKIN SAUCES.

All regions of Italy.

The name comes from the term *castello* ("castle") and *castellano* ("lord of the castle"), inspired by the long garments traditionally worn by nobles and princes.

Castellane, *a type of pasta of extraordinary elegance and beauty, capture the sauce to perfection. They were created by the die maker and Barilla designer Carlo Mori, and were introduced in 1987 in the Barilla* Esclusivi *line, along with* bifore, *with a B-shaped profile;* trifogli, *spaghetti with three grooves that help to speed up cooking; and* nicchiole, *which absorbs sauce beautifully and were inspired by the shape of mushrooms.*

SHORT DURUM WHEAT PASTA
Average size:
length 40.50 mm • diameter 16.50 mm • thickness 1.10 mm

CELLENTANI / WHOLE-GRAIN CELLENTANI

DRY, WITH FISH SAUCES.

Southern Italy.

This spring-shaped pasta owes its name to the Italian pop singer Adriano Celentano, dubbed, in his early days in the 1960s, "Molleggiato" (Springy), for his distinctive stage movements.

This hollow, spiral-shaped pasta was launched by Barilla in the 1960s. Cellentani are an evolution of fusilli bucati corti, with their characteristic grooved surface, suitable for absorbing rich fish sauces.

SHORT, HOLLOW DURUM WHEAT PASTA
Average size:
length 34.00 mm • diameter 5.80 mm • thickness 1.03 mm

CONCHIGLIE RIGATE

DRY, WITH SIMPLE, TOMATO OR MEAT SAUCES.

All regions of Italy. The large version is mainly used in Campania.

This pasta owes its name to its characteristic shell shape (or *conchiglia* in Italian). It is also known by other names in different areas of Italy, such as *abissini, arselle, cinesini, coccioline, conchigliette, tofarelle,* or *tofettine.* The larger version is known as *conchiglioni.*

There are dozens of shell-shaped pasta varieties known by the name conchiglie. *The origin of this pasta is thought to derive, as has often been the case throughout history, from a simple mistake, namely a die designed for a hollow pasta variety but having a slightly diagonal hole, leading to the production of tubes bent into the shape of a pipe or elbow. Once the mechanism was understood, the hole was further offset to produce a variety of* conchiglie: *smooth or ribbed, gently or deeply curved, big or small. The larger sized* conchiglie *can even be stuffed with vegetables, cheeses, and meats.*

Ironic references, symbols, and naturalistic memories are hidden among the pasta shapes, acccording to an amusing passage written by Cesare Marchi, taken from Quando siamo a tavola *(When We Are at the Table):* «*Pasta unleashes a waltz of metaphors in the mind... Some come from the world of zoology, such as* conchiglie *(shells),* conchigliette *(small shells),* chiocchiole *(snails),* creste di gallo *(cockscomb),* code di rondine *(dovetails),* occhi di elefante *(elephant's eyes),* vermicelli *(small worms),* lumaconi *(slugs),* linguine *(small tongues),* orecchiette *(small ears). Others from botany:* fiori di sambuco *(elderflowers),* gramigna *(common weed),* sedani *(celery)...* »
From: Marchi, Cesare, *Quando siamo a tavola,* Milan (I), Rizzoli, 1990.

SHORT DURUM WHEAT PASTA
Average size *conchiglie:*
length 18.50 mm • width 29.40 mm • thickness 1.25 mm
Average size *coquillettes:*
length 10.00 mm • diameter 3.25 • thickness 0.80 mm

FUSILLI / FUSILLI INTEGRALI / MINI FUSILLI

**DRY, WITH NEAPOLITAN-STYLE *RAGÙ*, MEAT SAUCES, AND RICOTTA CHEESE.
THE SHORT VERSIONS ARE ALSO SUITABLE FOR PASTA SALADS.**

*Central-southern Italy and Sardinia.
The industrial version is widespread throughout Italy.*

The homemade version consists of taking a strand of spaghetti, rolling it around a knitting needle, spacing it slightly to create a pasta coil. Industrial processing has also enabled the creation of a hollow version of *fusilli*. The name is derived from the Italian *fuso* ("spindle," a round wooden stick with tapered ends used to form and twist the yarn in hand-spinning) an instrument with a continuous rolling action reminiscent of the movement required to forge this pasta by hand. Available in various lengths, *fusilli* have an extraordinary variety of local names, confirming their wide use throughout Italy: known as *strangolapreti* in many regions, in Veneto and Friuli they are called *subioti*; in Abruzzo, Molise, and Lazio *ciufolitti* and *gnocchi col ferro*; and in Puglia, Basilicata, and Sardinia, *lombrichelli* and *maccheroni a ferrittus* (or similar expressions, with *ferro* taken to mean a knitting needle). In industrial production, in addition to official *fusilli*, other twisted pastas, such as *eliche*, *gemelli*, and *spirali* are often also referred to by the same name, sometimes creating confusion.

Fusilli have Arabic origins—they were first documented in the islands where the Muslim conquest of the Mediterranean began. They are known as busiati in Sicily and busi in Sardinia, terms deriving from the Arabic word bus, indicating the thin reed on which the pasta was rolled. This particular pasta-processing technique, documented in the fifteenth century using the term strangolapreti, became widespread first in central and southern Italy before becoming popular throughout the country.
Industrial production dates back to 1924, when the brothers Guido and Aurelio Tanzi, emigrants to New York, developed a machine they called Fusilla, which, for the first time, produced a type of pasta with a centered and perfectly regular hole.
Each region has its own varieties, with different names, sizes, and traditional sauces. In Sicily, it is served with a pesto typical of Trapani, while in Puglia and Lazio, the spread of sheep-farming favored lamb-based accompaniments. In Basilicata, where *fusilli with salami and horseradish was the highlight of Mardi Gras, this pasta was also believed to predict the sex of unborn children: a single strand, thrown into boiling water, predicted the birth of a male when it remained upright, and of a female when horizontal. In Calabria, tradition has it that a young girl risks becoming an old maid if she is unable to show her betrothed that she knows the 15 ways to cook pasta, with* fusilli *being the most important variety in this test.*

《...fusilli, filitelli, paternostri, lasagne, fettuccine, capelli d'angelo... On that day, the betrothed must set aside his love for the lady. With a stone in the place of his heart, he turns up at the bride-to-be's home—perhaps with his witness—in the guise of an uncompromising, unyielding examiner. He tastes this and that. How's the pasta? It seems a little overcooked. And the sauce? A little tasteless perhaps? A pinch of salt makes up for everything.... The girl holds out the dishes with a trembling hand.
The boy never lifts his eyes from his plate, not to be swayed, but you can well imagine the tragedy he is going through at that moment, the conflict between his heart and his stomach.》
From: Morbelli, Riccardo, *Il boccafina, ovvero il gastronomo avveduto*, Rome (I), Casini, 1967.

LONG OR SHORT, HOLLOW DURUM WHEAT PASTA
Average size of *fusilli*:
length 37.00 mm • diameter 9.65 mm • thickness 1.26 mm
Average size of *mini fusilli*:
length 26.00 mm • diameter 7.00 mm • thickness 1.00 mm

FARFALLE / MINI FARFALLE

DRY, WITH SIMPLE OIL, BUTTER, OR TOMATO ACCOMPANIMENTS, OR WITH CHEESE SAUCES. ALSO IDEAL FOR COLD SUMMER SALADS.

All regions of Italy. Particularly popular in Liguria.

The term is inspired by the wings of a butterfly (or *farfalla* in Italian), which the pasta resembles. This variety is also referred to as *stricchetti*, from a dialect form of the verb *stringere* ("to tighten"), referring to the central pinch, and *galani*, named after the bow-tie worn with a tuxedo. In Umbria, they are also called *fiocchetti*, again because of their resemblance to a bow-tie, and in Abruzzo and Puglia, nocchette, from the southern Italian term nocca, to indicate a knotted ribbon.

Farfalle conjure up, both in shape and in the imagination, the graceful multicolored creatures that hover in our gardens. Their large wings collect the sauce and retain it in the central fold, while the pinch offers a contrasting texture on the palate that enhances the condiments. Originally made from thin sheets of dough pinched by hand, they were once also called stricchetti.
Symbols and naturalistic memories are hidden among the pas-

ta shapes, acccording to an amusing passage written by Cesare Marchi: «*Pasta unleashes a waltz of metaphors in the mind: spaghetti, spaghettini, penne, pennoni, rigatoni, bucatoni, fidelini, trenette, tortiglioni. Some come from the world of zoology, such as farfalle (butterflies), farfalline (small butterflies).... Others from religion: capelli d'angelo (angel hair), maniche di frate (priest sleeves), avemmaria (Hail Mary), cappelli da prete (priest hats).*»
From: Marchi, Cesare, *Quando siamo a tavola*, Milan (I), Rizzoli, 1990.

**SHORT, PINCHED DURUM WHEAT PASTA
MADE FROM A SHEET OF DOUGH**
Average size of *farfalle*:
length 32.50 mm • width 24.00 mm • width 1.10 mm
Average size of *mini farfalle*:
length mm 22.50 • width 14.50 • width mm 0.90

GNOCCHETTI SARDI

SERVED MAINLY DRY, WITH FLAVORSOME MEAT AND SAUSAGE SAUCES AND SPRINKLED WITH PECORINO CHEESE. THIS PASTA IS ALSO OFTEN ENJOYED WITH CHOPPED FRESH TOMATOES AND BASIL, OR WITH TOMATO, RICOTTA, AND GRATED CHEESE.

Sardinia. The industrial version is widespread throughout Italy.

The term *gnocco* probably derives from the Venetian term *gnoco*, which in turn probably comes from the Langobard *knohha*—that is, "knuckle," or "tree knot." Many pastas, some quite dissimilar, are now known by the name of *gnocchi*, all of which were originally prepared from an irregular portion of dough, torn and rolled by hand, and then molded using just a fingertip. *Gnocchetto sardo*, in particular, is a small, ribbed pasta known, in the local dialect, as *malloreddus*, meaning "young calves or bulls," presumably from the Latin *malleolus*, a term already used by the ancient Romans to refer to a type of gnocchi.

This is an ancient pasta with Catalan origins, made with wheat flour colored with saffron. Gnocchetti sardi come in the shape of a dumpling with a hole in the center, or rather a large recess, like the gnocchi *found in other countries. In Sardinia they are called* malloreddus *or* macherones caidos, *and are flavored, according to some local recipes, with Pecorino cheese melted in a bain-marie (hot-water*

bath), *or with a sauce based on cream or on grated hard ricotta. Originally they were handmade, rubbing small discs of dough over a "comb" or loom heddle, and were traditionally served at engagement parties (where the betrothed would eat from the same plate), and at weddings.*

Antonio Frugoli (seventeenth century) from Lucca, in his work Pratica e scalcaria, *published in Rome in 1631, describes an official meal held in Madrid on 11 February 1625, comprising* «*maccheroni di Sardegna*», *now known as* gnocchetti sardi.
From: Frugoli, Antonio, *Pratica e scalcaria*, Rome (I), Francesco Cavalli, 1631. Vol. IV, p. 464.

SHORT DURUM WHEAT PASTA
Average size:
length 8.40 mm • width 8.40 mm • thickness 1.22 mm

GNOCCHI

DRY, WITH BUTTER AND CHEESE,
OVEN-BAKED WITH MEAT SAUCES, WITH
VEGETABLE SAUCES, AND IN SALADS.

Native to Lazio, and particularly typical of Rome. Being a basic pasta variety, it is also present, with slight variations, in Trentino, Friuli, Umbria, and Sardinia.

Extruded durum wheat flour (*semola*) gnocchi resemble a shell. *Gnocchi alla romana*, on the other hand, are made from semolina, are obtained by cutting the dough into diamonds or irregular fragments and are baked laid out as scales, slightly overlapped: they are commonly referred to as *gnocchi alla romana*. In Trentino and Friuli they are known as *canederli di Gries* and in Sardinia as *pillas*.

The term was historically used to indicate fragments or lumps of variously shaped dough, and in the Middle Ages and the Renaissance it became synonymous with pasta. Gnocchi made with semolina are probably a descendant of puls, *or cereal* polenta, *which was the main source of sustenance of the ancient Romans. Leftover* polenta *was cut up to prepare the* gnocchi *typical of the cuisine of Rome and the Lazio region in general—it was seasoned and then baked a second time in the oven. The extruded variety, now also known as* gnocchi, *takes the shape of a shell, the cavity of which envelops fresh sauces in summer and rich ones in winter.*

Ode alla farina, a Latin poem by the young historian Ludovico Antonio Muratori (1672–1750), cites gnocchi among other pasta shapes: «*Why do you open your eyes wide, O Muse? Why do you look with amazement at these macaroni sprinkled with cheese? They are the children of flour ... Ask the bakers, to whom they are so dear, and they will show you gnocchi, ravioli,...*».
From: Sada, Luigi, *Spaghetti e Compagni.* Edizioni del Centro Librario, Biblioteca de "La Taberna", Bari (I), 1982, pp. 45-46.

SHORT DURUM WHEAT PASTA
Average size:
length 16.50 mm • width 25.00 mm • thickness 1.28 mm

MEZZE MANICHE RIGATE

DRY, WITH FRESH TOMATO SAUCE
OR SIMPLY WITH BUTTER.

Mainly central and southern Italy.

This pasta owes the name *mezze maniche*, or "short sleeves," to its tubelike shape, available in different sizes and versions: *maniche di frate*, *maniche rigate*, *rigatoni*, or *bombardoni* (from the musical instrument known as a bombard). In Umbria and in the Marche it is called *moccolotti*, or "candle stubs," while in Campania the larger version is known as *pàccheri*, an onomatopoeic term for a "slap."

This pasta shape is very common in southern Italy, where it is often used, well dressed, in oven recipes au gratin, such as pies or casseroles. This is the case of the sbombata *from Umbria, in which a pan is lined with pastry, stuffed with pasta generously dressed with a giblet-and-grated-Pecorino sauce, covered with another layer of pastry, and baked in the oven.*

«*But, of course, first a plateful of vermicelli; without vermicelli, a lunch is not a lunch. How should we have them? With tomato sauce? Garlic and olive oil? Or 'alla marinara,' with olives and capers? I'd almost tell them to bring us half a portion of one, half of another, and half of stewed rigatoni. What do you say?...*»
From: Stefanile, Mario, *Invito ai Maccheroni*, Naples (I), Montanino, [1950], pp. 41-51.

SHORT, HOLLOW DURUM WHEAT PASTA
Average size:
length 24.00 mm • diameter 16.00 mm • thickness 1.15 mm

PUGLIA-STYLE ORECCHIETTE

DRY, TRADITIONALLY WITH TURNIP
GREENS, BUT ALSO WITH TOMATO
AND RICOTTA CHEESE.

*Central and southern Italy, especially Puglia and the region around Bari.
The industrial version is widespread throughout Italy.*

Orecchiette, or "small ears," to which shape they owe their name, are prepared by cutting up the dough (made from durum wheat flour and water) into pieces as large as beans. On a work surface these are then dragged with the tip of a finger or a knife to form a small shell with a very thin edge, which is subsequently turned inside out. They are called *orecchini* in Rome, *recchiatelle* in Campania, and *orecchia di prete* in Abruzzo and Basilicata. In their native Puglia, they are known by different names in different areas, depending on their size.

This is one of the oldest Italian pastas. The roughness of the central hollow absorbs the sauce to perfection.
Orecchiette *may have originated in Provence. The existence of a similar type of pasta in the south of France has been documented since the Middle Ages. Some historians believe that it was brought into Italy by the Angevins, a noble family of Frankish origin who* governed Puglia and Basilicata in the thirteenth century. Other historians argue that orecchiette, *which show a Middle Eastern influence, probably originated in the territory of Sannicandro di Bari, in Puglia, during the Norman-Swabian rule, between the twelfth and thirteenth centuries, and that they derive from a traditional Jewish recipe, brought to the region by a thriving Jewish community.*

**DURUM WHEAT PASTA MADE FROM DOUGH MOLDED
WITH A FINGERTIP, WITHOUT THE USE OF DIES; INDUSTRIALLY,
THEY ARE PRODUCED USING PUNCHES OR MOLDS**
Average size:
maximum diameter 23.00 mm • thickness 1.25 mm

PASTA MISTA, OR MIXED PASTA

USED MAINLY IN STOCK, MINESTRONE,
OR BEAN SOUP.

All regions of Italy.

As its name indicates, this is a mixture of different pasta shapes.

Mixed pasta was an "invention" of makers at the time when pasta was sold in bulk (i.e., until the 1950s). Retailers would mix portions of short pasta (or broken-up long pasta) with the same cooking times, left over in the bottom of their storage drawers. Today, it is made using dies that produce various shaped products with the same cooking times.

SHORT DURUM WHEAT PASTA
Average size:
maximum length 30.00 mm • thickness 1.15 mm

PENNE LISCE / PENNE RIGATE / PENNE MEZZANE / WHOLE-GRAIN PENNE RIGATE / MEZZE PENNE RIGATE / MINI PENNE RIGATE

DRY, SERVED SIMPLY WITH BUTTER OR WITH MEAT OR VEGETABLES. MEZZE PENNE GO WELL WITH MEAT, EGG, AND CHEESE SAUCES.

All regions of Italy.

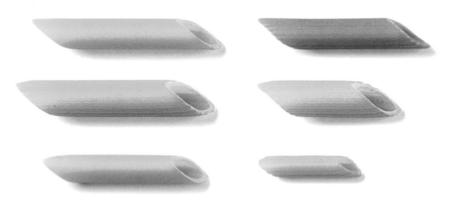

The Italian term *penne* refers to the quills once used for writing, cut on the bias to obtain a point. Indeed, this shape, obtained in either smooth or ribbed pasta tubes of varying lengths, reproduces the characteristic diagonal cut typical of quill pens. This type of pasta is also known as *mostaccioli, penne a candela, penne di ziti,* and *ziti tagliati.*

Penne *are one of the few pasta varieties with origins that can be traced back with certainty. In 1865, Giovanni Battista Capurro, a pasta maker from San Martino d'Albaro, in the province of Genoa, patented a machine that enabled fresh pasta to be cut diagonally, without crushing it, into the shape of 3-cm- or 5-cm-long quills (mezze penne or penne). The patent application document, kept in the Central State Archive of Rome, reads: "Until today, it was not possible to cut pasta diagonally other than with a pair of hand scissors, a method that, in addition to being too slow and wasteful, also has the drawback of producing an uneven cut and of crushing the pasta." Originally, penne, unlike other types of pasta, were traditionally colored with pure saffron, which gave them not only a different hue, but also a unique flavor. In Naples and Liguria, where penne are also known as* maccheroni, *a special smooth and extra-long variety known as* penne di Natale *(Christmas penne) is also produced for a traditional Christmas pie, in which it is used whole, without being broken up before cooking. In Sicily, perhaps due to the old tradition of cutting penne with scissors, penne di Natale are called* maltagliati *("badly cut") and served with a rich sauce, called* aggrassatu *(greased), made with onion, meat, and spices. Penne, in all their sizes, are one of the most widely consumed pastas in Italy.*

Cesare Marchi ironically recalls symbols and memories in an amusing passage on pasta taken from *Quando siamo a tavola* (When We Are at the Table): «*Pasta unleashes a waltz of metaphors in the mind: spaghetti, spaghettini, penne, pennoni, rigatoni, bucatoni, fidelini, trenette, tortiglioni. Some come from the world of zoology... Others from botany.* »
From: Marchi, Cesare, *Quando siamo a tavola,* Milan (I), Rizzoli, 1990.

SHORT DURUM WHEAT PASTA
Average size of *penne lisce*:
length 45.00 mm • diameter 7.30 • thickness 1.14 mm
Average size of *penne rigate*:
length 49.00 mm • diameter 8.85 mm • thickness 1.10 mm
Average size of *penne mezzane*:
length 40.00 mm • diameter 6.60 mm • thickness 1.10 mm
Average size of *pennette rigate*:
length 43.00 mm • diameter 7.70 mm • thickness 1.05 mm
Average size of mezze *penne rigate*:
length 35.00 mm • diameter 8.55 mm • thickness 1.10 mm
Average size of *whole-grain pennette*:
length 43.00 mm • diameter 7.70 mm • thickness 1.05 mm
Average size of *mini penne*:
length 34.00 mm • diameter 5.40 mm • thickness 0.92 mm

PIPE RIGATE / PIPETTE RIGATE / MINI PIPE RIGATE

USUALLY DRY, WITH TOMATO SAUCE, SIMPLE BUTTER-BASED CONDIMENTS, MEAT SAUCES, AND PEAS. THE SMALLER SHAPES ARE SERVED IN SOUPS OR STEWS.

All regions of Italy.

In Italian as in English, the term *pipe* recalls the instrument so dear to smokers, marked by a smooth curve that connects the stem to the tobacco chamber. *Pipe* are curved pasta tubes that take their name from this same elbow shape. They come in various sizes, known by other names such as *chifferi* (reminiscent of the Austrian *Kipferl*, or "croissant"), *chiocciolette, cirillini, genovesini, gobbetti, lumachine, stortini, tofarelle,* and *tortini.* This pasta also comes in a larger version.

Pipe, like conchiglie *and* lumachine, *form part of the category of elbow-shaped short pastas. For their production, the die makers insert a thin sheet of metal in the pipe through which the pasta is pushed. This obstructs the smooth flow of the pasta, causing greater pressure on one side than the other and forming a pipe-like curve. The shape of the* Kipfel—*a croissant prepared by seventeenth-century Austrian pastry makers to celebrate the victory of the national army against the Turks, who had advanced as far as the* gates of Vienna in 1682—seems to have influenced that of the pipe, also known as chifferi *and produced for centuries in pastry shops, where desserts were also prepared.*
This hollow pasta shape deftly picks up sauces and can contain small portions of meat or vegetables.

SHORT, HOLLOW DURUM WHEAT PASTA
Average size of *pipe rigate:*
length 27.00 mm • diameter 13 mm • thickness 1.10 mm
Average size of *pipette:*
length 17.00 mm • diameter 9.15 mm • thickness 1.00 mm
Average size of *mine pipe:*
length 15.00 mm • diameter 7.50 mm • thickness 0.84 mm

RIGATONI / MEZZI RIGATONI

DRY, WITH MEAT, VEGETABLE, OR SAUSAGE SAUCES. IT IS ALSO SUITABLE FOR BAKED DISHES, WITH MEAT SAUCES AND BÉCHAMEL.

Southern Italy, and as an industrial product, all regions of Italy.

The term originates from the *righe* ("ridges") that characterize the outer surface of this pasta, obtained through the incision of bronze dies. This shape is also known as *bombardoni, cannaroni rigati, maniche, trivelli* (from *trivella,* or "auger"), and *tufoloni rigati.*

This pasta was made possible by the invention of a grooved die, designed to make the dough more porous and suitable to picking up the condiment. The texture and size of the shape, whether big or small, makes it ideal in the richly seasoned savory baked dishes particularly popular in southern Italy. In Lazio, in Roviano, rigatoni have been given the imaginative and very special name of scorzasellari, *because of their characteristic streaking resembling that of a celery stalk (from* scorza, *or "peel," and* sellare, *or "celery").*

《*Until recently, scientists had told us that eating pasta was bad for our health. Now, however, they have publicly stated that pasta is the ideal dietary food. And so, in Paris and in London, everyone is eating spaghetti and rigatoni. It took some time for these know-alls to learn that which was already known to Pulcinella, who asked for nothing more than to eat macaroni every day.*》
From: Giaquinto, Adolfo, *Gli scienziati e gli spaghetti,* Rome (I), 1911.

SHORT, HOLLOW DURUM WHEAT PASTA
Average size of *rigatoni:*
length 45.00 mm • diameter 14.10 mm • thickness 1.05 mm
Average size of *mezzi rigatoni:*
length 20.00 mm • diameter 14.10 mm • thickness 1.05 mm

SEDANI RIGATI / SEDANINI RIGATI

DRY, WITH TOMATO SAUCE, WITH MEAT, OR WITH BUTTER. ALSO SUITABLE FOR BAKED DISHES.

All regions of Italy.

The name derives from the Italian word *sedano*, or "celery," the stem of which is vaguely reminiscent of the streaked and slightly curved shape of this pasta. Available in various sizes, *sedani* are also known as *cannolicchi*, *cornetti*, *diavoletti*, *fagiolini*, *folletti*, *gnocchetti di ziti*, *gramignoni*, *maccheroncini*, *stortini*, and *tubetti lunghi*.

Sedani *and* sedanini, *named after celery, are characterized by their grooves in relief, which absorb the sauce to perfection, thus making the dish tastier.*

SHORT, HOLLOW DURUM WHEAT PASTA
Average size of *sedani rigati*:
length 43.00 mm • diameter 8.80 mm • thickness 1.10 mm
Average size of *sedanini rigati*:
length 34.00 mm • diameter 5.70 mm • thickness 1.05 mm

TORTIGLIONI / WHOLE-GRAIN TORTIGLIONI

DRY, WITH MEAT, SAUSAGE, OR VEGETABLE SAUCES. ALSO SUITABLE FOR BAKED DISHES.

Specialty from southern Italy, in particular Campania, now popular across the country.

Tubes of pasta with twisted grooves. As with *rigatoni*, the name refers to the pasta's outer appearance, obtained through the incision of dies. The name derives from the vulgar Latin term *tortillare*, a deformation of the classical Latin word *torquere*, or "twist."

This pasta owes its name to its twisted, tubelike shape. Once upon a time, the name tortiglioni, *which indicated an object twisted into a spiral, was used for a pasta that is more similar to our* fusilli *of today, and mentioned in the mid-fourteenth-century* Libro della mensa *("Refectory Book") kept by the Priors of Florence.*

SHORT DURUM WHEAT PASTA
Average size:
length 43.00 mm • diameter 11.60 mm • thickness 1.10 mm

LIGURIAN TROFIE

DRY, BOILED IN WATER WITH GREEN BEANS
AND POTATOES AND SEASONED WITH
THE CLASSIC PESTO SAUCE, MADE WITH
LIGURIAN BASIL, GARLIC, PINE NUTS, SALT,
PECORINO CHEESE, AND LIGURIAN OIL.

*Liguria and the adjacent coastal areas of Tuscany
and as an industrial production, all regions of Italy.*

Originating in Liguria, *trofie* feature a spiral or curled shape. This pasta, made with flour, a little bran, and water, is formed into small pieces the size of a bean. These are rubbed on a work surface with the palms of both hands, so as to obtain short spiral-shaped spaghetti with pointed ends. The pasta is also sometimes rolled around a thin knitting needle. The name of this distinctive pasta is thought to derive from the Genoese dialect term *strofissià*, meaning "to rub," recalling the movement performed by the housewife to prepare this stretched and twisted dumpling. Trofie are sometimes also called *rechelline*, probably from the name of the town of Recco, near Genoa, where they are a local specialty.

This handmade pasta from Liguria, made from durum wheat flour and water, is originally from Recco, a town on the region's eastern coastline, traditionally served with pesto sauce.
The trofie are one of the many regional pastas created from mixing flour, water, and other ingredients such as stale bread, potatoes, and (in the Apennine mountain areas) even chestnuts. The ingredients that enrich the basic flour-and-water mixture are used to give

extra softness to this pasta, still served today with the traditional basil and Pecorino cheese pesto. The now rare version that included chestnuts in the dough was served with a melted-cheese sauce typical of the mountain regions.
Legend has it that the birth of trofie is linked to the Crusades, when the ships' cooks would knead flour and water to prepare the pasta and, on cleaning their floured hands, would set aside any dough tra-e-die (between their fingers) to prepare another dish.

There is an ancient saying in Genoa:
No capì ûnna trofia, meaning "To not understand a *trofia*,"
《 *To not understand a thing.* 》

SHORT DURUM WHEAT PASTA
Average size:
length 41.00 mm • width 4.90 mm • thickness 1.20 mm

SICILIAN CASARECCE WITH ARTICHOKE SAUCE

PREPARATION: 45 minutes
COOKING TIME: 20 minutes
DIFFICULTY: EASY

4 SERVINGS

12 oz. (350 g) Barilla
Sicilian casarecce
5-6 artichokes
Juice of 1 lemon
1/4 cup (50 ml) dry white wine
1/4 cup (50 ml) vegetable broth
1/2 cup plus 2 tbsp. (60 g) grated
Parmigiano Reggiano cheese
2 tbsp. (40 ml) extra-virgin olive oil
1 clove garlic, chopped
1 tbsp. parsley, chopped
Salt and pepper to taste

Clean artichokes by slicing at least 1/4 inch (0.5 cm) off the tops and bottoms and removing all the tough outer leaves. Cut the artichokes in half lengthwise and remove the chokes. Cut into thin slices and soak in a bowl of water with the lemon juice to prevent the artichokes from turning black. Bring a pot of salted water to a boil for the pasta.

Meanwhile, in a skillet, heat olive oil over medium and add the artichokes, garlic, and parsley. Season with salt and pepper and stir to combine. Add the white wine, raise the heat to medium-high, and cook until the wine evaporates completely. Add the vegetable broth and cook for about 10 minutes. Cook the Sicilian casarecce in the pot of boiling salted water until it is al dente; drain. Toss the pasta with the artichoke sauce and grated Parmigiano Reggiano.

ALTERNATIVE VERSIONS
The sauce in this recipe is ideal for short pasta shapes. You can choose shapes such as penne rigate, gemelli, and sedani rigati, or lisci instead of casarecce.

I ❤ Pasta

SICILIAN CASARECCE
WITH ANCHOVIES AND FENNEL

PREPARATION: 25 minutes
COOKING TIME: 10 minutes
DIFFICULTY: MEDIUM

4 SERVINGS

12 oz. (350 g) Barilla
Sicilian casarecce
7 oz. (200 g) anchovies, rinsed,
cleaned, and filleted
2 tbsp. (30 ml) extra-virgin olive oil
1 1/2 oz. (40 g) dried apricots, sliced
3/4 oz. (20 g) pine nuts
3/4 oz. (20 g) pistachio nuts
1 oz. (30 g) parsley, chopped
2 stalks wild fennel, chopped
1 clove garlic
Fresh breadcrumbs for topping,
as needed
Salt and pepper to taste

Bring a pot of salted water to a boil for the pasta.

Heat 1 tablespoon oil in a nonstick pan and toast the breadcrumbs.

Heat the remaining 1 tablespoon oil in a large pan over medium heat
and add the whole peeled garlic clove. Add the anchovies and continue
cooking for 1 to 2 minutes, then add the apricots and cook for an
additional 1 minute. Add the chopped fennel, the pine nuts, and the
pistachios and cook for 30 seconds, then remove from heat. Remove
the garlic clove. Season with salt and pepper.

Cook the Sicilian casarecce in the boiling salted water until it is al dente;
drain. Toss with the anchovy sauce. Sprinkle with a bit of toasted
breadcrumbs and chopped parsley and serve.

ALTERNATIVE VERSIONS
For this regional recipe, a regional
shape such as Sicilian casarecce
is ideal. However, as an alternative
you can use pennette lisce,
sedani lisci, and rigatoni.

CASTELLANE WITH CARAMELIZED CHERRY TOMATOES, GOAT CHEESE, AND TOASTED PINE NUTS

PREPARATION: 1 hour
COOKING TIME: 1 1/2 hours
DIFFICULTY: MEDIUM

4 SERVINGS

12 oz. (350 g) Barilla castellane
7 oz. (200 g) cherry tomatoes, preferably Pachino
1 1/2 oz. (40 g) goat cheese
1 oz. (30 g) spring onion, thinly sliced
3/4 oz. (20 g) pine nuts, or about 2 1/2 tbsp.
2 tbsp. (30 ml) extra-virgin olive oil
1 tbsp. plus 2 tsp. (15 g) brown sugar
Zest of 1 lemon
Fresh thyme leaves to taste
Salt to taste

Heat the oven to 210°F (100°C).

Arrange the tomatoes in a baking dish, season with salt, and drizzle with half of the olive oil. Sprinkle with the brown sugar, thyme leaves, and lemon zest and bake in the oven for about 1 hour.

Bring a pot of salted water to a boil for the pasta.

Meanwhile, heat the remaining oil in a large pan over low and sauté the spring onion for about 10 minutes. Add the caramelized tomatoes and season with salt.

Toast the pine nuts in a nonstick pan over medium heat until they are golden and fragrant, about 5 minutes.

Cook the castellane in the pot of boiling salted water until it is al dente; drain. Transfer pasta to the pan with the tomatoes. Add the goat cheese and the pine nuts and stir to combine. Serve hot.

ALTERNATIVE VERSIONS
You can replace the castellane with other short pastas, such as mezze maniche rigate, fusilli, and tortiglioni.

I ♥ Pasta

CASTELLANE WITH PARMA HAM AND BALSAMIC VINEGAR

PREPARATION: 15 minutes
COOKING TIME: 15 minutes
DIFFICULTY: EASY

4 SERVINGS

12 oz. (350 g) Barilla castellane
10 slices Parma ham
1/3 cup (30 g) grated
Parmigiano Reggiano cheese
1/2 oz. (15 g) unsalted butter
Balsamic vinegar, preferably of
Modena, as needed
1 tbsp. chopped fresh thyme
Salt to taste

Bring a pot of salted water to a boil for the castellane.

Julienne the slices of ham. Melt the butter in a pan over medium heat and sauté the Parma ham for about 2 minutes, then add the balsamic vinegar.

Cook the castellane in the pot of boiling salted water until it is al dente. Drain, reserving some of the cooking water. Toss pasta with the sauce, stirring in the grated Parmigiano Reggiano and a little of the cooking water to bind the ingredients. Sprinkle with the chopped thyme and serve.

ALTERNATIVE VERSIONS
This dish is perfect with short pastas, such as farfalle and penne rigate, or with egg garganelli.

I ♥ Pasta

CELLENTANI WITH PEARS, GORGONZOLA, AND WALNUTS

PREPARATION: **30 minutes**
COOKING TIME: **10 minutes**
DIFFICULTY: **EASY**

4 SERVINGS

12 oz. (350 g) Barilla cellentani
4 oz. (120 g) Gorgonzola, cubed
2 pears (choose firm varieties such as Anjou or Bosc, which stand up to cooking)
8 walnut pieces
2 sprigs thyme
Lemon juice, as needed
Salt and pepper to taste

Peel, core, and dice the pears. Sprinkle them with lemon juice so that they do not oxidize.

Bring a pot of salted water to a boil and cook the cellentani until it is al dente; drain.

Remove thyme leaves from stems; discard stems.

Toss pasta in a pan with the Gorgonzola, the pear, the walnuts, and the thyme leaves for a few minutes over low heat. Season with salt and pepper and serve immediately.

ALTERNATIVE VERSIONS
This is a recipe that lends itself perfectly to short pasta shapes, such as farfalle, gnocchi, and conchiglie rigate.

WHOLE-GRAIN CELLENTANI MEDITERRANEAN SALAD

PREPARATION: 15 minutes
COOKING TIME: 10 minutes
DIFFICULTY: EASY

4 SERVINGS

12 oz. (350 g) Barilla
whole-grain cellentani
7 oz. (200 g) plum tomatoes
2 3/4 oz. (80 g) red bell pepper,
seeded and cubed
2 3/4 oz. (80 g) yellow bell pepper,
seeded and cubed
2 3/4 oz. (80 g) cucumber, seeded
and cubed
1 3/4 oz. (50 g) celery, diced
1 3/4 oz. (50 g) peas
3 1/2 oz. (100 g) fresh fava beans
1 1/2 oz. (40 g) red onion
(preferably Tropea onion), peeled
and chopped
1 3/4 oz. (50 g) black olives
3/4 oz. (20 g) capers
1/3 cup (80 ml) extra-virgin olive oil
Oregano (fresh leaves or dried) to
taste, for garnish
Salt to taste

ALTERNATIVE VERSIONS

Other short pasta shapes, even if
not whole grain, are ideal for this
recipe. In addition to cellentani,
you can use penne rigate, farfalle,
and fusilli.

Bring a pot of salted water to a boil and cook the whole-grain cellentani until barely al dente. Drain and rinse with cold running water.

Transfer pasta to a large bowl and toss with a drizzle of olive oil so that the pasta does not stick together.

Blanch the peas for 1 minute in a saucepan of boiling water and plunge them immediately in ice water to stop the cooking process. Repeat blanching process with the fava beans, then peel them.

Drain capers and olives, reserving brining liquid.

Clean and wash all of the vegetables, peel the onion and the cucumber and remove the cucumber's seeds. Cut everything into small cubes.

Combine all the ingredients with the cellentani. Add a pinch of salt and the olive oil, and serve. Garnish with a dusting of oregano, to taste.

I ♥ Pasta

CONCHIGLIE RIGATE WITH SPECK, GORGONZOLA, AND HAZELNUTS

PREPARATION: 15 minutes
COOKING TIME: 12 minutes
DIFFICULTY: EASY

4 SERVINGS

12 oz. (350 g) Barilla conchiglie rigate
5 oz. (150 g) speck, sliced
3 1/2 oz. (100 g) Gorgonzola cheese, diced
2 3/4 oz. (80 g) hazelnuts, coarsely chopped
1/3 cup (40 g) grated Parmigiano Reggiano cheese
Salt and pepper to taste

Cut the speck into strips about 1/10-inch (2-3-mm) wide and sauté it in a nonstick pan without oil, until crispy. Set aside.

Bring a pot of salted water to a boil and cook the conchiglie rigate until it is al dente. Drain, reserving some of the cooking water.

Meanwhile, melt the Gorgonzola in a pan over low heat, adding a bit of the pasta cooking water to thin it. Add the grated Parmigiano Reggiano and season with salt and pepper.

Toss the pasta with the sauce in the pan and stir in the hazelnuts.

Sprinkle the pasta with the crispy speck and serve.

ALTERNATIVE VERSIONS
This sauce also goes perfectly with farfalle, cellentani, penne rigate, and mezze maniche rigate.

CONCHIGLIE RIGATE SALAD WITH TUNA AND SESAME

PREPARATION: 30 minutes
COOKING TIME: 13 minutes
DIFFICULTY: EASY

4 SERVINGS

12 oz. (350 g) Barilla
conchiglie rigate
7 oz. (200 g) red onion, peeled
1/2 cup (150 ml) red wine
5 oz. (150 g) yellow bell pepper,
seeded and cut into
1/2-inch (1-cm) dice
9 oz. (250 g) fresh tuna
5 oz. (150 g) cooked borlotti
(cranberry) beans
1/3 cup (80 ml) extra-virgin olive oil
3 sprigs thyme
Fresh chile pepper, seeded and
finely diced, as needed
Sesame seeds, as needed
Salt and pepper to taste

Bring a pot of salted water to a boil and cook the conchiglie rigate until just al dente. Drain pasta and rinse with cold running water. Transfer to a large bowl and toss with a drizzle of olive oil so that the pasta does not stick together.

Meanwhile, toast the sesame seeds in a nonstick pan over medium heat for 3 to 5 minutes, shaking pan occasionally.

Peel and cut the onion into wedges and cook it in a pan with the red wine, salting lightly. Let it cool.

Heat a few tablespoons of olive oil in a pan and sauté the yellow pepper until crisp-tender. Season with salt.

Cut the tuna into 2/3-inch (2-cm) cubes, season with salt and pepper, and sauté in a pan with the remaining oil for a few minutes (it should remain pink). Dredge the tuna in the sesame seeds.

Toss the conchiglie rigate with the yellow pepper, beans, tuna, onion, and the chile pepper. Garnish with the thyme and some sesame seeds.

ALTERNATIVE VERSIONS
This sauce also goes very well with farfalle, rigatoni, and Sicilian casarecce.

FARFALLE / SHORT PASTA

FARFALLE WITH TOMA CHEESE AND MUSHROOMS

PREPARATION: 30 minutes
COOKING TIME: 20 minutes
DIFFICULTY: EASY

4 SERVINGS

12 oz. (350 g) Barilla farfalle
14 oz. (400 g) porcini mushrooms (ceps)
4 1/2 oz. (125 g) Toma cheese (or other soft cow's-milk cheese, such as Brie)
1/3 cup (75 ml) milk; more as needed
2 tbsp. (30 ml) extra-virgin olive oil
3/4 oz. (20 g) parsley, chopped
1 tbsp. (20 ml) dry white wine
1 clove garlic, chopped
Salt and pepper to taste

Bring a pot of salted water to a boil for the pasta.

Bring the milk to a boil in a saucepan. Add the Toma and stir until the cheese is melted and a smooth fondue is obtained. If necessary, dilute with more milk. Season with salt and keep warm.

Scrub and slice the mushrooms.

Heat the oil in a skillet over medium heat and sauté the garlic and parsley. Add the mushrooms and cook for about 5 minutes. Add the white wine and season with salt and pepper.

Cook the farfalle in the salted boiling water until it is al dente; drain. Transfer to the pan with the mushroom mixture. Add the cheese sauce, toss to combine, and cook for 1 to 2 minutes more.

ALTERNATIVE VERSIONS
Gnocchi and rigatoni, as well as other short pasta shapes, such as pipe rigate, are excellent with this recipe.

I ♥ Pasta

FARFALLE WITH FRESH TUNA, TOMATO, AND TAGGIASCA OLIVES

PREPARATION: 30 minutes
COOKING TIME: 20 minutes
DIFFICULTY: EASY

4 SERVINGS

12 oz. (350 g) Barilla farfalle
1 1/3 lbs. (600 g) tomatoes
9 oz. (250 g) fresh tuna
3 1/2 oz. (100 g) leeks, finely chopped
3 1/2 oz. (100 g) carrot, finely chopped
3 1/2 oz. (100 g) celery, finely chopped
1/4 cup (50 ml) extra-virgin olive oil
1 3/4 oz. (50 g) Taggiasca olives (or other small black olives)
3 sprigs marjoram
Salt and pepper to taste

Prepare the tomatoes by making an X-shaped incision on the bottom of each tomato and blanching it in boiling water for 10 to 15 seconds. Immediately dip the tomatoes in ice water, then peel, seed, and cut them into cubes.

Heat half the olive oil in a skillet and sauté the leeks, carrot, and celery. Add the tomatoes and a pinch of salt. Cook for 5 minutes, then add the olives.

Bring a pot of salted water to a boil and cook the farfalle until al dente.

Meanwhile, cut the tuna into 1-inch (3-cm) cubes, season with salt and pepper, and sauté in a pan with the remaining oil for 3 to 4 minutes (it should remain pink). Transfer the tuna to the vegetable sauce.

Drain the pasta and toss it with the sauce. Garnish with the marjoram leaves.

ALTERNATIVE VERSIONS
With this sauce, other shapes of short pasta also match well: conchiglie rigate, cellentani, and castellane.

FARFALLE SALAD WITH STEAMED OCTOPUS AND SAUTÉED SHRIMP

PREPARATION: 40 minutes
COOKING TIME: 1 hour 15 minutes
DIFFICULTY: EASY

4 SERVINGS

12 oz. (350 g) Barilla farfalle
11 oz. (300 g) octopus
3 1/2 oz. (100 g) jumbo shrimp, peeled and deveined
3 1/2 oz. (100 g) cherry tomatoes, preferably Pachino
1 3/4 oz. (50 g) celery, or about 2 stalks, diced
2 tbsp. (40 ml) extra-virgin olive oil
1/4 oz. (10 g) fresh basil leaves, hand torn, or about ½ cup
1 clove garlic, minced
Salt and white pepper to taste

Bring a pot of salted water to a boil and cook the farfalle until it is al dente. Drain and rinse with cold running water.

Wash and clean the octopus, removing the ink sack and internal organs by making a circular cut around the beak with a paring knife and pulling it free (the organs will come with it). Steam in a steamer basket until tender when pierced with a fork (45 minutes to 1 hour). Let cool and then dice the octopus.

Heat 1 tablespoon of oil in a skillet over high heat and sauté the shrimp just until cooked through, 1 to 2 minutes. Put the octopus and shrimp in a bowl, then add the garlic, the basil, the tomatoes, the celery, and the remaining olive oil and mix well. Season with salt and white pepper, add the farfalle, and toss to combine. Refrigerate for at least 30 minutes. Serve at room temperature.

ALTERNATIVE VERSIONS
This fish sauce is also excellent with other short pastas, such as whole-grain pennette rigate, farfalle, and fusilli.

I ♥ Pasta

MINI FARFALLE WITH PUMPKIN PURÉE

PREPARATION: **40 minutes**
COOKING TIME: **40 minutes**
DIFFICULTY: **EASY**

4 SERVINGS

12 oz. (350 g) Barilla mini farfalle
1 3/4 lb. (800 g) pumpkin
7 oz. (200 g) potatoes, peeled
and diced
1 3/4 oz. (50 g) onion, peeled
and sliced
2 tbsp. (30 ml) extra-virgin olive oil
6 cups (1.5 l) vegetable broth
2 sprigs rosemary, plus more
for garnish
Salt and pepper to taste

Heat the olive oil in a large pan and sauté the onion and the rosemary sprig, previously washed and drained.

Cut open the pumpkin, scoop out and discard the seeds and inner membrane, and peel. Dice pumpkin into large piece. Add the pumpkin and the potatoes to the pan with the onion and sauté lightly, then add the broth. Season with salt and pepper, and cook until tender, about 25 minutes.

Meanwhile, bring a pot of salted water to a boil for the mini farfalle. Transfer pumpkin mixture to a blender or food processor and purée.

Cook the mini farfalle in the pot of boiling salted water until it is al dente; drain. Toss with the pumpkin purée. Garnish with fresh rosemary.

ALTERNATIVE VERSIONS
This delicate soup is also excellent with other small pastas, such as mini farfalle, mini pipe rigate, and mini fusilli.

I ♥ Pasta

FUSILLI WITH TUNA

PREPARATION: 30 minutes
COOKING TIME: 35 minutes
DIFFICULTY: EASY

4 SERVINGS

12 oz. (350 g) Barilla fusilli
1 lb. 2 oz. (500 g) tomatoes, peeled and chopped
7 oz. (200 g) canned tuna in oil, drained and flaked
3 1/2 oz. (100 g) onion, peeled and chopped
2 tbsp. (30 ml) extra-virgin olive oil
4 fresh basil leaves, coarsely chopped
1 tbsp. minced fresh parsley
1 clove garlic
Salt and pepper to taste

Heat the olive oil in a pan and sauté the onion with the whole garlic clove. When the onion has turned golden brown, add the tomatoes, then season with salt and pepper. Cook the sauce over high heat for about 15 minutes, stirring occasionally. Add the tuna and cook for another 4 to 5 minutes. Remove the garlic clove, and add the minced parsley and the chopped basil.

Bring a pot of salted water to a boil and cook the fusilli until it is al dente; drain. Toss with the tomato sauce, and serve.

ALTERNATIVE VERSIONS

This recipe also works well with short pasta. Instead of fusilli, you can use farfalle, penne rigate, and conchiglie rigate.

FUSILLI
WITH GARDEN VEGETABLES

PREPARATION: 40 minutes
COOKING TIME: 13 minutes
DIFFICULTY: EASY

4 SERVINGS

12 oz. (350 g) Barilla fusilli
1/4 cup (50 ml) extra-virgin olive oil
1 3/4 oz. (50 g) leeks, white parts
only, sliced
1 3/4 oz. (50 g) eggplant
1 3/4 oz. (50 g) zucchini, diced
1 3/4 oz. (50 g) red bell pepper,
seeded and diced
1 3/4 oz. (50 g) yellow bell pepper,
seeded and diced
2 oz. (60 g) pumpkin, peeled
and diced
1 oz. (25 g) peas
1 3/4 oz. (50 g) carrot, diced
1 3/4 oz. (50 g) celery, diced
5 oz. (150 g) tomatoes, peeled,
seeded, and diced
6 fresh basil leaves,
coarsely chopped
Salt to taste

ALTERNATIVE VERSIONS
For this light and colorful sauce,
a short pasta shape, including
whole-grain pasta, is ideal. Instead
of fusilli, you can use mezze penne
rigate, farfalle, or sedani rigati.

Dice the eggplant or cut it into matchsticks, then put it in a colander, salt it lightly, and allow it to drain for about 30 minutes.

Bring a pot of salted water to a boil for the pasta.

Boil the peas in a pot of lightly salted water until tender.

Heat the olive oil in saucepan and sauté the leeks, celery, and carrot until tender. Add (in order of their cooking time) the peppers, eggplant, pumpkin, and zucchini, plus salt to taste. Add the tomatoes and cook for 5 minutes. Finally, add the basil.

Cook the fusilli in the salted boiling water until al dente; drain. Toss with the vegetable sauce and serve.

I ♥ Pasta

WHOLE-GRAIN FUSILLI WITH ASPARAGUS CREAM SAUCE

PREPARATION: 30 minutes
COOKING TIME: 20 minutes
DIFFICULTY: EASY

4 SERVINGS

12 oz. (350 g) Barilla
whole-grain fusilli
1 lb. (450 g) asparagus
1/2 cup (100 ml) heavy cream
1 cup (100 g) grated
Parmigiano Reggiano cheese
1 oz. (30 g) shallots, peeled
and sliced
1 tbsp. (15 ml) extra-virgin olive oil
Salt

Remove the hard ends of the asparagus and cut all the stalks to the same length. Set aside the asparagus tips and slice the stalks.

Heat the oil in a frying pan and gently sauté the shallots until brown. Add the asparagus slices to the shallots and sauté for 2 minutes. Cover with water and cook for about 15 minutes. Salt lightly. Transfer asparagus mixture to a blender and purée.

In a pan of boiling water, blanch the asparagus tips for 3 to 4 minutes, then plunge in ice water to stop the cooking process.

Bring a large pot of salted water to a boil and cook the fusilli until al dente; drain. In a large pan, toss the pasta with the asparagus purée. Add the asparagus tips, the heavy cream, and the grated Parmigiano Reggiano, then stir together and cook over low heat for 1 minute before serving.

ALTERNATIVE VERSIONS
For this recipe, it is best to use a short pasta—even if it isn't whole grain—that binds well with the sauce. For example: penne rigate, farfalle, and mezze maniche rigate.

WHOLE-GRAIN FUSILLI WITH MUSHROOMS, BRESAOLA, AND ARUGULA

PREPARATION: 50 minutes
COOKING TIME: 20 minutes
DIFFICULTY: EASY

4 SERVINGS

12 oz. (350 g) Barilla whole-grain fusilli
7 oz. (200 g) button mushrooms
3 1/2 oz. (100 g) bresaola, cut in thin strips
1 cup (200 ml) heavy cream
1 3/4 oz. (50 g) arugula
1/3 cup (40 g) grated Parmigiano Reggiano cheese
2 tbsp. (30 ml) extra-virgin olive oil
3 1/2 oz. (100 g) tomato purée
1/3 cup (20 g) parsley, chopped
1 clove garlic
Salt and pepper to taste

Bring a large pot of salted water to a boil for the pasta.

Heat a pan with the oil over medium heat. Sauté the whole peeled garlic clove, the mushrooms, and the parsley for 2 minutes. Season with salt and pepper.

Add the bresaola and cook for a few seconds. Add the tomato purée and cook for 5 minutes over high heat.

Add the heavy cream, reduce the heat to medium-low, and let the sauce reduce for 2 to 3 minutes. Season with salt and pepper.

Meanwhile, cook the pasta in the salted boiling water until al dente; drain. Toss the pasta with the sauce and the arugula (reserving a few leaves for garnish, if desired), and sauté for a few minutes. Sprinkle with the grated Parmigiano Reggiano and garnish with a few leaves of uncooked arugula or cooked mushroom slices.

ALTERNATIVE VERSIONS

In addition to whole-grain fusilli, this recipe goes perfectly with other shapes of short pasta, with whole grain as an option: rigatoni, farfalle, penne rigate, and pennette rigate.

I ♥ Pasta

MINI FUSILLI
WITH HAM AND PEA PURÉE

PREPARATION: 15 minutes
COOKING TIME: 25 minutes
DIFFICULTY: EASY

4 SERVINGS

12 oz. (350 g) Barilla mini fusilli
1 lb. 2 oz. (500 g) peas
3 1/2 oz. (100 g) ham, cubed or cut
into strips
2 tbsp. (30 ml) extra-virgin olive oil
1 oz. (30 g) onion, peeled and sliced
2 cups (500 ml) water
Salt to taste

Brown the onion in a pan with the oil, then add the peas and sauté for 2 minutes. Add the 2 cups (500 ml) (or enough to cover) water and cook for about 15 minutes, stirring occasionally.

Set aside 1 tablespoon peas. Transfer the onions and remaining peas to a blender and purée until creamy. Return the pea purée to the pan.

Bring a pot of salted water to a boil and cook the mini fusilli until al dente; drain. Transfer to the pan with the pea purée, adding the reserved peas and the ham. Season with salt.

Toss to combine over low heat, cook for 1 minute, and serve.

ALTERNATIVE VERSIONS
This delicate green sauce goes perfectly with small pasta shapes. Instead of mini fusilli, you can use mini farfalle and mini penne rigate.

GNOCCHETTI SARDI WITH MULLET AND SAFFRON

PREPARATION: 40 minutes

COOKING TIME: 25 minutes

DIFFICULTY: HIGH

4 SERVINGS

12 oz. (350 g) Barilla gnocchetti sardi
8 medium-size red mullet
1 potato, peeled and diced
1/2 stalk celery, finely diced
1/2 medium carrot, peeled and finely diced
1/4 medium onion, peeled and finely diced
1 pinch saffron (0.0044 oz./125 mg)
1 sprig rosemary
1 medium tomato
1 oz. (30 g) unsalted butter
1 1/2 tbsp. (20 ml) extra-virgin olive oil
2/3 cup (150 ml) heavy cream
Salt and freshly ground pepper to taste

Scale, gut, fillet, and rinse the red mullet.

Melt the butter in a skillet over medium heat and fry the potato, celery, carrot, and onion for a few minutes.

Add the heavy cream and the saffron to the vegetable mixture and bring to a boil. Cook for a few minutes, season with salt and pepper, and keep sauce warm.

Prepare the tomatoes by making an X-shaped incision on the bottom of the tomato and blanch it in boiling water for 10 to 15 seconds. Immediately dip the tomato in ice water, then peel and dice it. Set aside.

Finely chop the rosemary needles. In a separate pan, fry them in the oil over low heat. Add the mullet and brown quickly on both sides. When the fish fillets are well browned, remove them from the heat and keep warm, then add the saffron sauce to the pan with the fish.

Bring a pot of salted water to a boil and cook the gnocchetti sardi until it is al dente; drain. Gently toss the pasta with the saffron sauce, tomatoes, and the mullet.

ALTERNATIVE VERSIONS

Three other shapes of short pasta that you can use in the place of gnocchetti sardi are conchiglie rigate, pipe rigate, and castellane.

GNOCCHI WITH ARUGULA PESTO

PREPARATION: 15 minutes
COOKING TIME: 14 minutes
DIFFICULTY: EASY

4 SERVINGS

12 oz. (350 g) Barilla gnocchi
4 oz. (120 g) arugula
6 1/2 oz. (180 g) ripe tomatoes
1 oz. (25 g) ParmigianoReggiano
cheese, grated
1/4 oz. (10 g) whole shelled
almonds, plus more for garnish
5 tbsp. (70 ml) extra-virgin olive oil
(preferably from Liguria)
1/4 clove garlic
Salt to taste

Prepare the tomatoes by making an X-shaped incision on the bottom of each tomato and blanching it in boiling water for 10 to 15 seconds. Immediately dip the tomatoes in ice water, then peel them and cut them into cubes.

Rinse and dry the arugula. Pulse it in a blender with the olive oil, a pinch of salt, the garlic, and the almonds. Add the grated Parmigiano Reggiano, then the tomatoes, and pulse to blend.

Bring a pot of salted water to a boil and cook the gnocchi until they are al dente; drain. Transfer to a bowl and mix with the arugula pesto, adding a bit of the pasta water and a drizzle of olive oil to adjust the thickness.

Garnish with chopped almonds, if desired.

ALTERNATIVE VERSIONS
Instead of gnocchi, you can choose another type of short pasta for this fragrant and tasty sauce, such as gemelli or trofie liguri.

I ♥ Pasta

MEZZE MANICHE RIGATE WITH LOBSTER, CARAMELIZED CHERRY TOMATOES, AND ZUCCHINI

PREPARATION: 1 hour

COOKING TIME: 1 1/2 hours

DIFFICULTY: HIGH

4 SERVINGS

12 oz. (350 g) Barilla mezze maniche
rigate
1 lobster, about 1 1/3 lb. (600 g)
3/4 oz. (20 g) onion, peeled
3/4 oz. (20 g) carrot
3/4 oz. (20 g) celery
7 oz. (200 g) sweet cherry tomatoes,
such as Datterini
7 oz. (200 g) zucchini, finely diced
1/3 cup (80 ml) extra-virgin olive oil
2 cups (1/2 l) water
1 oz. (30 g) pine nuts
3 tbsp. cane sugar
1 bunch fresh herbs (sage,
rosemary, thyme, parsley, and basil)
3/4 oz. (20 g) fresh parsley, chopped
1 red chile pepper
1 clove garlic, halved
Salt to taste

ALTERNATIVE VERSIONS

Other pasta shapes can be used
for this dish: bavette and spaghetti
for long pasta, or pennette lisce for
short pasta.

Bring a large pot of water to a boil. Cook lobster for 2 minutes. Cut the lobster in half and remove the meat from the shell. Cut off claws and crack open. Remove meat from claws and cut meat into bite-size pieces. Cut off lobster tail. Cut tail crosswise into 4 pieces each. Cut each lobster body in half lengthwise. Remove the coral (bright-orange part) and tomalley (greenish part); finely chop. Make a light fish stock (which will be used to finish cooking the pasta): Place the celery, carrot, onion, and the bunch of herbs (reserving some thyme leaves and the parsley stems) in a pot; add the lobster shells and scraps; and sauté well with a drizzle of olive oil for about 5 minutes. Add about 2 cups (500 ml) (or enough to cover) water and simmer. Arrange the tomatoes in a baking dish and add the sugar, 2 tablespoons olive oil, and a scattering of fresh thyme leaves. Season with salt and bake at 210°F (100°C) for about 1 hour, until tender and caramelized. Meanwhile, toast the pine nuts in a pan, tossing lightly to toast evenly. Set aside.

In a hot pan, fry the garlic halves and the parsley stems in 2 tablespoons olive oil for a few seconds, then add the finely chopped lobster meat and salt lightly. When cooked, transfer the lobster to a large bowl, leaving the garlic and parsley stems in the pan.

In the same pan, cook the diced zucchini with the remaining oil, halved garlic, and parsley stems; after about 5 minutes, add the cooked lobster meat and mix well. Bring a pot of salted water to a boil and cook the mezze maniche rigate for only half the time indicated for al dente on the package instructions; drain. Return the pasta to the pot over medium heat, add the lobster-and-zucchini sauce and add the fish stock a little at a time, until the pasta is cooked to al dente. When the pasta is almost cooked, add the caramelized tomatoes and stir to combine. To serve, arrange the mezze maniche on a plate and garnish with the chopped parsley, the caramelized cherry tomatoes, and the pine nuts.

I ♥ Pasta

PUGLIA-STYLE ORECCHIETTE WITH BROCCOLI RAAB

PREPARATION: 15 minutes
COOKING TIME: 13 minutes
DIFFICULTY: EASY

4 SERVINGS

12 oz. (350 g) Barilla Puglia-style orecchiette
11 oz. (300 g) broccoli raab
1/4 cup (60 ml) extra-virgin olive oil
2 anchovy fillets in olive oil, rinsed
1 clove garlic, thinly sliced
1 dried chile pepper, seeded and chopped
Salt and freshly ground pepper to taste

In a large shallow pan, heat 3 tablespoons of oil. Add the garlic, chile pepper, anchovies, and 3 or 4 tablespoons of water and cook until the anchovies have disintegrated. Remove pan from the heat.

Meanwhile, bring a pot of salted water to a boil for the orecchiette.

Peel and trim the broccoli raab, discarding any wilted leaves. Cook the pasta and the broccoli raab together in the boiling salted water until the orecchiette is al dente. A few minutes before draining the orecchiette, reheat the anchovy mixture. Drain the orecchiette with a fine-mesh strainer, if possible, so as not to lose small pieces of the broccoli raab. Transfer orecchiette and broccoli raab to the pan with the anchovy sauce and toss to thoroughly combine. Add remaining 1 tablespoon of oil, season with freshly ground pepper, toss, and serve immediately.

ALTERNATIVE VERSIONS
This dish is perfect with short pastas, such as mezze maniche rigate, penne rigate, and tortiglioni.

I ♥ Pasta

PUGLIA-STYLE ORECCHIETTE WITH CHERRY TOMATOES, OLIVES, AND EGGPLANT

PREPARATION: 20 minutes
COOKING TIME: 15 minutes
DIFFICULTY: EASY

4 SERVINGS

12 oz. (350 g) Barilla
Puglia-style orecchiette
1 eggplant, peeled and medium
diced
10 ripe cherry tomatoes, quartered
3 1/2 oz. (100 g) small black olives
(preferably Taggiasca), pitted
6 tbsp. (80 ml) extra-virgin olive oil
2 sprigs rosemary, chopped
1 clove garlic
Salt and black pepper to taste

Put the eggplant in a colander, salt it lightly and allow it to drain for about 30 minutes.

In a large shallow pan over medium heat, toss the eggplant with the oil, a dash of black pepper, and the whole garlic clove. Add the cherry tomatoes and cook for 5 minutes. Halve the olives and add them to the sauce. Remove the garlic clove. Add the rosemary and stir to combine.

Bring a large pot of salted water to a boil and cook the orecchiette until it is al dente; drain. Toss pasta with the sauce and serve.

ALTERNATIVE VERSIONS
This dish is perfect with short pastas, such as mezze maniche rigate, penne rigate, and tortiglioni.

PASTA MISTA WITH BROCCOLI CREAM SAUCE AND CROUTONS

PREPARATION: 20 minutes

COOKING TIME: 9 minutes

DIFFICULTY: EASY

4 SERVINGS

9 oz. (250 g) Barilla pasta mista
18 oz. (500 g) broccoli,
cut into florets
1 1/3 lb. (600 g) potatoes, peeled
and chopped
3 1/2 oz. (100 g) onion, peeled
and sliced
6 cups (500 ml) water
2 oz. (60 g) day-old bread, cubed
2 tsp. (10 ml) extra-virgin olive oil
Salt and pepper to taste

Place the vegetables in a saucepan, cover with water, and cook until tender. Transfer to a blender and purée, diluting with water, if needed. Season with salt and pepper.

Return broccoli sauce to the pan and bring to a boil. Add the pasta mista to the sauce and cook, adding a little water if necessary, until the pasta is al dente.

Heat a little olive oil in a pan and sauté the bread cubes. Garnish the pasta mista in broccoli cream sauce with croutons and serve.

ALTERNATIVE VERSIONS

This broccoli cream sauce is also excellent with other pastas, such as ditali lisci, pennette lisce, and Neapolitan ziti, broken into smaller pieces.

I ♥ Pasta

PENNE LISCE "MARI E MONTI" (SEA AND MOUNTAINS)

PREPARATION: 20 minutes
COOKING TIME: 30 minutes
DIFFICULTY: EASY

4 SERVINGS

12 oz. (350 g) Barilla penne lisce
20 prawns or jumbo shrimp
5 oz. (150 g) tuna or swordfish fillet, cut into small cubes
7 oz. (200 g) button mushrooms
1 clove garlic, chopped
3/4 oz. (20 g) fresh parsley, chopped
3 1/2 oz. (100 g) tomatoes, seeded and diced
1/4 cup (60 ml) extra-virgin olive oil
Salt and pepper to taste

Scrub, rinse, and slice the mushrooms. Clean and shell the prawns or shrimp (if you prefer, you can leave some unshelled).

Meanwhile, heat 2 tablespoons of oil in a pan, add the tuna (or swordfish) and prawns (or shrimp), season with salt and pepper, and stir-fry for 2 minutes. Transfer to a bowl and set aside.

Bring a pot of salted water to a boil and cook the penne lisce until it is al dente. Drain, reserving a little pasta water.

Heat the remaining 2 tablespoons of oil in the same pan used for the seafood and sauté the garlic. Before the garlic begins to brown, add the mushrooms and cook for 2 minutes. Add the tomatoes and cook for another 2 minutes, adding a little of the pasta water, if necessary. Add the seafood and stir to combine.

Toss the pasta with the seafood sauce, sprinkle with the chopped parsley, and serve.

ALTERNATIVE VERSIONS
Instead of penne lisce, you can also use penne mezzane, sedani lisci, or gnocchi.

I ♥ Pasta

PENNE MEZZANE WITH VEGETABLES AND CACIOCAVALLO CHEESE

PREPARATION: 40 minutes
COOKING TIME: 45 minutes
DIFFICULTY: EASY

4 SERVINGS

12 oz. (350 g) Barilla
penne mezzane
1 3/4 oz. (50 g) carrot
1 3/4 oz. (50 g) yellow and
red peppers
2 medium eggplants
3 1/2 oz. (100 g) fresh tomatoes
3 1/2 oz. (100 g) zucchini
1/2 cup (50 g) grated
Parmigiano Reggiano cheese
5 oz. (150 g) Caciocavallo cheese
(or provolone cheese), diced
1 tsp. parsley, chopped
2 tbsp. (30 ml) extra-virgin olive oil
Vegetable oil for frying, as needed
Salt and pepper to taste

For the béchamel
2 cups (500 ml) milk
1 1/2 oz. (40 g) unsalted butter
1/3 cup (40 g) all-purpose flour
Grated nutmeg to taste
Salt to taste

ALTERNATIVE VERSIONS
Instead of penne mezzane, you
can also choose other short pasta
shapes: sedani lisci, ditaloni lisci,
and penne lisce.

Cut 1 eggplant into slices about 1/10 inch (3 mm) thick, using a mandoline. Place the slices in a colander, salt lightly, and allow to drain for 20 minutes. Heat at least 1/2 inch of vegetable oil in a pan until hot and shimmering. Fry the eggplant.

Dice the other eggplant, the carrot, peppers, tomatoes, and zucchini. Sauté them in a pan with a drizzle of olive oil and the parsley, salt, and pepper. Meanwhile, prepare the béchamel: Melt the butter in a heavy-bottomed pan. To make a roux, add the flour and whisk butter and flour together for 3 to 4 minutes over low heat, until smooth.

Heat the milk in a separate pan, then add to the roux, pouring it in a slow stream. Adjust the salt, season with a bit of nutmeg, and continue cooking, whisking constantly to avoid the formation of lumps, until the sauce is thick and creamy. If the béchamel is too thick, add a bit of milk. If it is too thin, let it cook for a few additional minutes.

Heat the oven to 365°F (185°C). Bring a pot of salted water to a boil and cook the penne mezzane until 1 to 2 minutes before the time indicated for al dente. Mix penne with the vegetables, the béchamel, and the Caciocavallo.

Line a baking pan with the fried eggplant slices, arrange the pasta-and-vegetable mixture on top, and sprinkle with the grated Parmigiano Reggiano. Bake for 15 to 20 minutes, or until golden brown. Run a knife around the edge of the pan and invert pan over a serving plate so that vegetable crust is on top.

I ♥ Pasta

PENNE RIGATE ALL'ARRABBIATA

PREPARATION: 30 minutes
COOKING TIME: 25 minutes
DIFFICULTY: EASY

4 SERVINGS

12 oz. (350 g) Barilla penne rigate
1 lb. 6 oz. (600 g) tomatoes, peeled and chopped
2 tbsp. (30 ml) extra-virgin olive oil
2 cloves garlic, thinly sliced
Red chile pepper, fresh or dried (or crushed red pepper flakes), to taste
Salt to taste

Heat the olive oil in a large skillet and and lightly sauté the garlic, adding some chile pepper to taste. (If you are using a fresh chile, seed and slice it; dry chile can be crumbled by hand, using disposable gloves.)

Once the garlic and chile have softened, add the tomatoes, season with salt, and continue cooking for about 15 minutes, stirring occasionally.

Meanwhile, bring a large pot of salted water to a boil and cook the penne rigate until it is al dente; drain. Toss the pasta with the tomato sauce and serve.

ALTERNATIVE VERSIONS This traditional Sicilian dish can also be made with short pastas such as tortiglioni and rigatoni.

PENNE RIGATE ALLA NORMA

PREPARATION: 1 hour
COOKING TIME: 30 minutes
DIFFICULTY: MEDIUM

4 SERVINGS

12 oz. (350 g) Barilla penne rigate
2 1/4 lb. (1 kg) plum
tomatoes, chopped
9 oz. (250 g) eggplant
1 3/4 oz. (50 g) onion, peeled and
roughly chopped
1 3/4 oz. (50 g) salted hard ricotta
cheese (ricotta salata), grated
2 tbsp. (30 ml) extra-virgin olive oil
6 fresh basil leaves, shredded
1 clove garlic
All-purpose flour, as needed
2 tbsp. extra-virgin olive oil, plus
more for frying eggplant
Salt and pepper to taste

Cut the eggplant into cubes, then put it in a colander, salt it lightly, and allow it to drain for about 30 minutes. In a large frying pan, heat about 1/2 inch of oil over medium heat. Lightly flour the eggplant and fry it, in batches if necessary, until golden brown. Drain on paper towels.

Bring a large pot of salted water to a boil for the penne rigate.

Heat the 2 tablespoons of oil in a large frying pan over medium heat and sauté the onion with the whole garlic clove until softened. Add the tomatoes. Season with salt and pepper, and cook, stirring occasionally, for about 10 minutes. Run mixture through a vegetable strainer. Add the fried eggplant to the tomato sauce and keep warm.

Cook the penne rigate in the pot of boiling salted water until it is al dente; drain. Toss pasta with the sauce and the shredded basil. Sprinkle with the ricotta and serve.

ALTERNATIVE VERSIONS
This traditional Sicilian dish can also be made with short pastas such as tortiglioni and rigatoni.

WHOLE-GRAIN PENNETTE RIGATE WITH CHERRY TOMATOES, CAPERS, OLIVES, AND MONKFISH

PREPARATION: 20 minutes
COOKING TIME: 20 minutes
DIFFICULTY: MEDIUM

4 SERVINGS

12 oz. (350 g) Barilla whole-grain pennette rigate
11 oz. (300 g) monkfish
2 tbsp. (30 ml) extra-virgin olive oil
7 oz. (200 g) cherry tomatoes, quartered
1/2 cup (100 ml) white wine
1 3/4 oz. (50 g) small black olives (preferably Taggiasca), pitted
1/4 oz. (10 g) capers
1 salted anchovy, rinsed, filleted, and chopped
1 clove garlic
1 tbsp. (4 g) chopped fresh parsley
Salt to taste

Clean, fillet, and chop the monkfish.

Bring a pot of salted water to a boil for the pennette rigate.

Meanwhile, heat the oil in a pan with the whole garlic clove, then add the fish and sauté for a few seconds. Add the white wine and cook until it evaporates. Add the tomatoes and stir to combine. Add the anchovy and the capers and cook for a few minutes. Add a little water if necessary. Add the olives and season with salt. Stir to combine.

Cook the pennette rigate in the pot of boiling salted water until it is al dente; drain. Toss pasta with the sauce, sprinkle with chopped parsley, and serve.

ALTERNATIVE VERSIONS
Both regular and whole-grain tortiglioni, cellentani, and farfalle go perfectly with this sauce.

I ♥ Pasta

WHOLE-GRAIN PENNETTE RIGATE WITH SAUSAGE, CABBAGE, AND SMOKED SCAMORZA CHEESE

PREPARATION: 20 minutes
COOKING TIME: 16 minutes
DIFFICULTY: MEDIUM

4 SERVINGS

12 oz. (350 g) Barilla whole-grain pennette rigate
7 oz. (200 g) sausage
5 oz. (150 g) savoy cabbage, sliced
1/4 cup (50 ml) extra-virgin olive oil
2 oz. (60 g) smoked Scamorza cheese, cubed
1 oz. (30 g) Parmigiano Reggiano cheese, grated
1 clove garlic
1 sprig of rosemary, chopped
Salt and pepper to taste

Remove sausage casing and crumble the sausage. Heat the oil in a skillet over medium heat and sauté the sausage, the whole garlic clove, and the rosemary. Add the cabbage and a little water, cover pan and braise gently over low heat for about 5 minutes. Remove the garlic clove and season with salt and pepper.

Bring a large pot of salted water to a boil and cook the whole-grain pennette rigate until it is al dente; drain. Transfer pasta to the sauce and toss to combine. Stir in the grated Parmigiano Reggiano and top with the smoked Scamorza.

ALTERNATIVE VERSIONS
We recommend short pastas for this dish, such as rigatoni, penne rigate, and whole-grain tortiglioni.

I ♥ Pasta

MEZZE PENNE RIGATE WITH CLAMS AND CHICKPEAS

PREPARATION: 1 hour
SOAKING TIME: 12 hours
COOKING TIME: 1 hour 15 minutes
DIFFICULTY: MEDIUM

4 SERVINGS

12 oz. (350 g) Barilla mezze penne rigate
3 1/2 oz. (100 g) dried chickpeas (or 9 oz. [250 g] cooked chickpeas)
1 3/4 oz. (800 g) clams
1/4 cup (60 ml) extra-virgin olive oil
3/4 oz. (20 g) parsley, chopped
4-5 basil leaves, rinsed, dried, and cut into fine strips
1 clove garlic
Chile pepper to taste
Salt and black pepper to taste

If using dried chickpeas, soak the chickpeas in water for about 12 hours.

Put soaked chickpeas in a pot of cold water, bring to a boil, and cook for about 1 hour or until tender. Meanwhile, scrub and rinse the clams. Heat 1 1/2 tablespoons olive oil in a pan and sauté the whole garlic clove, chile pepper to taste, and chopped parsley until garlic is browned. Add the clams and cook until they open, discarding any that do not open. Once they have opened, filter the cooking liquid and discard some of the shells.

Bring a pot of salted water to a boil for the pasta. Mash the cooked chickpeas with a fork (or blend them, if you prefer a creamier texture), and thin the purée with a bit of the clam juice and the remaining 1 1/2 tablespoons oil, then season with a pinch of salt and dash of black pepper.

Boil the mezze penne rigate in the boiling salted water until it is al dente; drain. Toss penne with the chickpea purée and then toss with the clams in the pan. Sprinkle with the basil leaves and serve.

ALTERNATIVE VERSIONS
For this sauce, which brings together seafood and legumes, you can also use other forms of short pasta, such as mezze maniche rigate, rigatoni, and penne rigate.

MINI PENNE RIGATE WITH ZUCCHINI AND CHERRY TOMATOES IN PARMIGIANO REGGIANO BASKETS

PREPARATION: 20 minutes
COOKING TIME: 20 minutes
DIFFICULTY: MEDIUM

4 SERVINGS

12 oz. (350 g) Barilla mini penne rigate
3 1/2 oz. (100 g) zucchini, or about 1/2 medium
1 1/2 oz. (40 g) small black olives, preferably Taggiasca, pitted
1 oz. (30 g) salt-packed capers, rinsed
9 oz. (250 g) cherry tomatoes, preferably Pachino, seeded and diced
3/4 oz. (20 g) white onion, peeled and finely chopped
1 tbsp. (20 ml) extra-virgin olive oil
1/2 oz. (15 g) pine nuts
1 bunch herbs (such as oregano and basil), chopped
1 tbsp. minced fresh parsley
1 clove garlic
1/4 lb. (120 g) Parmigiano Reggiano cheese, grated
Salt and crushed red pepper to taste

ALTERNATIVE VERSIONS

This dish is also excellent with other pastas, such as mini fusilli, mezze penne rigate, and pennette rigate.

Heat the olive oil in a pan over medium and sauté the onion. Add the whole garlic clove and the tomatoes and stir. Add the herbs, the olives, and the capers, cook for a few minutes, and season with salt. Toast the pine nuts in a hot pan for a few minutes, tossing or stirring occasionally, until golden and fragrant.

Make 4 Parmigiano Reggiano baskets: Heat a nonstick skillet over medium-low, remove from heat, and sprinkle with one-quarter of the grated cheese. Return it to heat until the cheese has completely melted. Make a basket by resting the resulting hot cheese wafer on an inverted cup, such as a coffee cup (this must be done very quickly, before the cheese cools completely). Repeat until you have made 4 baskets. Set aside.

Bring a pot of salted water to a boil and cook the mini penne rigate, along with the zucchini, until the pasta is al dente (and the zucchini crisp-tender). Drain the pasta and zucchini. Remove the garlic clove from the sauce. Transfer the pasta and zucchini to the pan with the sauce and stir to combine. Season with salt and crushed red pepper.

Place the pasta inside the Parmigiano Reggiano baskets, sprinkle with the toasted pine nuts, and serve.

PIPE RIGATE
WITH SCALLOPS AND PUMPKIN

PREPARATION: 40 minutes
COOKING TIME: 10 minutes
DIFFICULTY: EASY

4 SERVINGS

12 oz. (350 g) Barilla pipe rigate
11 oz. (300 g) pumpkin
12 scallops
4 tsp. (20 ml) extra-virgin olive oil
3 cups (750 ml) water
1 yellow onion, peeled and chopped
1 sprig rosemary, chopped
1 clove garlic, chopped
Balsamic vinegar (preferably of Modena), optional
Salt and pepper to taste

Cut the pumpkin in half with a serrated knife. Scrape out and discard seeds and any loose fibers from inside pumpkin. Peel one half of the pumpkin and cut into a 1/2-inch (1-cm) dice; set aside. Put the other half of the pumpkin in a large pot with the chopped onion and a pinch of salt. Add the 3 cups (750 ml) (or enough to cover) water, bring it to a boil, and cook the vegetables until they are tender when pierced with a fork, 20 to 25 minutes. Drain, reserving the cooking water. Let pumpkin cool, then scoop out pumpkin flesh and transfer, with the onion, to a food processor or blender and carefully blend until creamy. If mixture is too thick, add some of the reserved cooking water.

Rinse the scallops, pat dry, and dice. Heat the oil in a pan over medium heat with the garlic and the rosemary, then sauté the diced pumpkin, seasoning with salt and pepper. Set the diced-pumpkin mixture aside. In the same pan, sauté the scallops for 1 minute on each side, season with salt and pepper, then add the pumpkin cream and the sautéed diced-pumpkin mixture. Meanwhile, bring a pot of salted water to a boil and cook the pipe rigate until it is al dente; drain. Toss with the creamy pumpkin sauce, add the diced-pumpkin mixture and the scallops, and stir to combine. Serve drizzled with a few drops of balsamic vinegar, if desired.

ALTERNATIVE VERSIONS
This recipe is also excellent with sedani rigati, conchiglie rigate, and mezze maniche rigate.

VEGETARIAN-STYLE MINI PIPE RIGATE

PREPARATION: 40 minutes

COOKING TIME: 20 minutes

DIFFICULTY: EASY

4 SERVINGS

12 oz. (350 g) Barilla mini pipe rigate
12 oz. (350 g) tomatoes, peeled and chopped
1/4 cup (50 ml) extra-virgin olive oil
1 3/4 oz. (50 g) onion
1 3/4 oz. (50 g) eggplant
1 3/4 oz. (50 g) zucchini
1 oz. (25 g) peas
1 3/4 oz. (50 g) carrot
1 3/4 oz. (50 g) celery
4 fresh basil leaves
Salt to taste

Dice the eggplant, then put it in a colander, salt it lightly, and allow it to drain for about 30 minutes.

Dice the carrot, celery, and zucchini. Wash and dry the basil, then roughly chop.

Boil the peas.

Peel and chop the onion, then brown it in a pan with the oil along with the celery and carrots.

Add all the diced vegetables, according to their various cooking times, and season with salt.

Add the peeled and chopped tomatoes and cook for another 10 minutes.

Meanwhile, bring a pot of salted water to a boil and cook the mini pipe rigate until it is al dente; drain. In a large bowl, toss the pasta with the vegetable sauce. Sprinkle with the basil and serve.

ALTERNATIVE VERSIONS
This colorful and delicious sauce goes well with small pastas. In addition to the mini pipe rigate, you can also use mini fusilli or mini penne rigate.

PIPETTE RIGATE SOUP WITH POTATOES AND CHESTNUTS

PREPARATION: 20 minutes
SOAKING TIME: 12 hours
COOKING TIME: 1 hour 30 minutes
DIFFICULTY: EASY

4 SERVINGS

7 oz. (200 g) Barilla pipette rigate
7 oz. (200 g) dried chestnuts
9 oz. (250 g) potatoes, peeled and diced
1 3/4 oz. (50 g) leek, white part only, finely sliced
3 1/2 oz. (100 g) onion, peeled and finely sliced
1 1/4 oz. (35 g) unsalted butter
4 cups (1 l) vegetable broth
2 cups (500 ml) milk
1 tbsp. (20 ml) extra-virgin olive oil
Salt and pepper to taste

Soak the dried chestnuts in cold water for 12 hours; drain.

Melt the butter in a large pan over medium, and sauté the leek and the onion until softened. Add the potatoes and the chestnuts, and sauté briefly.

Add the broth and the milk, season with salt and pepper, and cook over low heat for about 1 1/4 hours. Then either leave the soup chunky or blend it.

Add the pipette rigate directly to the soup and cook until it is al dente (about 8 minutes). Serve the soup with a drizzle of olive oil.

ALTERNATIVE VERSIONS
This typically autumnal soup is perfect with other pastas, such as ditaloni rigati and farfalline.

I ♥ Pasta

TIMBALE OF PIPETTE RIGATE WITH ZUCCHINI, CARROTS, AND CHERRY TOMATOES IN CREAMY GORGONZOLA SAUCE

PREPARATION: 50 minutes
COOKING TIME: 25 minutes
DIFFICULTY: MEDIUM

4 SERVINGS

9 oz. (250 g) Barilla pipette rigate
2 zucchini, diced
2 carrots, diced
3 1/2 oz. (100 g) cherry tomatoes, preferably Pachino, peeled and quartered; plus more for garnish (optional)
1/4 oz. (10 g) unsalted butter for the molds
2 oz. (60 g) Gorgonzola cheese
1/2 cup (100 ml) milk
1/3 cup (30 g) grated Parmigiano Reggiano cheese
2 tbsp. minced fresh parsley
2 tbsp. extra-virgin olive oil, plus more for drizzling
1 sheet phyllo pastry, defrosted
Salt and pepper to taste
Fresh herbs to taste (optional)

ALTERNATIVE VERSIONS

This timbale can also be prepared with other pasta, such as spaghetti, egg taglierini, and mini penne rigate.

Butter 4 aluminum timbale molds. Cut the sheet of phyllo into quarters and line the molds with the pastry dough.

Bring a pot of salted water to a boil and cook the pipette rigate for half the recommended cooking time for al dente; drain. Toss pasta with a drizzle of olive oil in a bowl and let cool.

Heat the olive oil in a pan and sauté the zucchini and carrots for about 4 minutes; season with salt and pepper. Add the tomatoes and cook for 1 minute more.Heat the milk in a saucepan over low heat. Add the Gorgonzola, allow it to melt, and season with salt and pepper. Heat the oven to 350°F (180° C).

Toss the pipette rigate with the tomato-zucchini-and-carrot sauce and divide evenly among the molds. Sprinkle with the Parmigiano Reggiano and bake for 5 minutes. Spread a thin layer of Gorgonzola cream on 4 individual dishes and invert the timbales in the center. Garnish with cherry tomatoes or fresh herbs, if desired.

RIGATONI CACIO E PEPE

PREPARATION: 10 minutes
COOKING TIME: 11 minutes
DIFFICULTY: EASY

4 SERVINGS

12 oz. (350 g) Barilla rigatoni
1/2 cup (100 ml) extra-virgin olive oil
2 1/4 cup (200 g) grated Pecorino Romano cheese
Salt and coarsely ground black pepper

Bring a pot of salted water to a boil and cook the rigatoni until it is al dente.

Meanwhile, mix the Pecorino with the olive oil and 2 to 3 tablespoons of the pasta water in a bowl.

Season with salt and with either a light or generous sprinkling of freshly ground black pepper, to taste.

Drain pasta, then toss with Pecorino mixture and serve hot.

ALTERNATIVE VERSIONS
This traditional recipe from Lazio is also excellent with bucatini and spaghetti alla chitarra.

I ♥ Pasta

MEZZI RIGATONI AND BEANS

PREPARATION: 1 hour
SOAKING TIME: 12 hours
COOKING TIME: 20 minutes
DIFFICULTY: EASY

4 SERVINGS

7 oz. (200 g) Barilla mezzi rigatoni
11 oz. (300 g) dried cannellini beans
11 oz. (300 g) dried borlotti
(cranberry) beans
7 oz. (200 g) onion, chopped
3 1/2 oz. (100 g) carrots, or about 2
small, chopped
3 1/2 oz. (100 g) celery, or about 2
stalks, chopped
2 tbsp. (30 ml) extra-virgin olive oil
1 sprig fresh thyme
Salt and pepper to taste

Soak the beans in cold water overnight; drain.

Heat the olive oil in a pan over medium. Sauté the vegetables until crisp-tender, then add the beans and thyme.

Add enough cold water to just cover the mixture and bring to a boil.

Reduce heat and simmer for about 1 hour, then add salt and pepper and the mezzi rigatoni. Let the pasta cook for about 10 minutes. Serve.

ALTERNATIVE VERSIONS
Other soup pastas can be used to make this delicious bean dish, such as ditaloni rigati and farfalline.

I ♥ Pasta

MEZZI RIGATONI WITH PORCINI MUSHROOMS AND THYME OVER GORGONZOLA FONDUE

PREPARATION: 30 minutes
COOKING TIME: 20 minutes
DIFFICULTY: MEDIUM

4 SERVINGS

12 oz. (350 g) Barilla mezzi rigatoni
14 oz. (400 g) porcini mushrooms (ceps), diced large
5 oz. (150 g) Gorgonzola cheese
1 oz. (30 ml) heavy cream
1/2 cup (50 g) grated Parmigiano Reggiano cheese
1 oz. (30 g) roughly chopped nuts (such as pistachios, hazelnuts, or pine nuts), toasted
1 tbsp. (20 ml) extra-virgin olive oil
1 bunch parsley, leaves and stems chopped separately
1 bunch thyme, leaves, chopped
1 clove garlic
Salt and white pepper to taste

In a preheated pan, add the olive oil with the parsley stems and whole garlic clove; then add the mushrooms and sauté them over high heat for a few minutes, until well browned. Remove and discard the parsley stems and the garlic clove. Season with salt and white pepper, then add the chopped thyme and parsley leaves.

Bring a pot of salted water to a boil for the pasta.

Meanwhile, in a skillet, melt the Gorgonzola over low heat with the heavy cream. When the mixture is completely melted, add the grated Parmigiano Reggiano and season with salt. Blend the mixture and continue to simmer.

Cook the mezzi rigatoni in the pot of boiling salted water until al dente; drain. Transfer the pasta to the pan with the mushrooms and toss for a few seconds.

On a flat serving plate, spread the Gorgonzola fondue in a thin layer and place the pasta in the center. Garnish with the toasted nuts and serve.

ALTERNATIVE VERSIONS

For this recipe, other shapes of pasta are also excellent, including long shapes like egg tagliatelle, as well as short shapes such as castellane and tortiglioni.

I ♥ Pasta

SEDANI RIGATI WITH TOMATO PESTO

PREPARATION: 5 minutes
COOKING TIME: 10 minutes
DIFFICULTY: EASY

4 SERVINGS

12 oz. (350 g) Barilla sedani rigati
12 oz. (800 g) ripe tomatoes
2/3 cup (60 g) grated
Parmigiano Reggiano cheese
1 oz. (30 g) pine nuts
1 oz. (30 g) almonds
1 oz. (30 g) walnuts
3 tbsp. (45 ml) extra-virgin olive oil
5 fresh mint leaves
1 clove garlic, crushed
Salt and pepper to taste

Prepare the tomatoes by making an X-shaped incision on the bottom of each tomato and blanching it in boiling water for 30 to 40 seconds. Remove the tomatoes with a slotted spoon and reserve the water to cook the pasta. Immediately dip the tomatoes in ice water, then peel, seed, and cut them into quarters.

Put the tomatoes, pine nuts, almonds, walnuts, garlic, mint leaves, Parmigiano Reggiano, and 2 tablespoons of olive oil into a blender. Blend thoroughly, until the mixture is smooth; season with salt and pepper.

Bring the tomato cooking water back to a boil, add a pinch of salt, and cook the sedani rigati until it is al dente. Meanwhile, pour the pesto into a large dish. Drain the pasta and transfer it to the dish with the pesto; add the remaining 1 tablespoon of oil and mix well. Serve in individual portions, with a drizzle of olive oil and a dash of pepper.

ALTERNATIVE VERSIONS
This Mediterranean dish is ideal with short pastas, such as pennette rigate, fusilli, and conchiglie rigate.

SEDANI RIGATI SALAD WITH PARMA HAM

PREPARATION: 15 minutes
COOKING TIME: 6 minutes
DIFFICULTY: MEDIUM

4 SERVINGS

11 oz. (300 g) Barilla sedani rigati
7 oz. (200 g) Parma ham, in one slice
7 oz. (200 g) pickled vegetables
1/4 cup (60 g) mayonnaise
1 tbsp. (15 g) mustard
1/4 cup (50 ml) extra-virgin olive oil
1 tsp. (5 g) chopped fresh parsley
1/2 lemon
Salt and pepper to taste

Bring a pot of salted water to a boil for the sedani rigati.

Meanwhile, mix the mayonnaise and mustard in a bowl with a drizzle of oil and a sprinkle of pepper. Dice the ham, then drain and chop the pickled vegetables.

Peel the lemon: using a very sharp knife, remove all the peel, including the white pith and the membrane on each segment. Then finely dice the peel.

Cook the sedani rigati in the pot of boiling salted water until it is barely al dente. Drain pasta and rinse with with cold running water.

Transfer the pasta to a large bowl and add the mustard sauce, ham, pickled vegetables, parsley, and lemon. Season with salt and pepper, stir to combine, and add a drizzle of oil.

ALTERNATIVE VERSIONS
Other short pastas can also be used to make this appetizing dish, such as penne rigate, fusilli, and farfalle.

I ♥ Pasta

SEDANINI RIGATI WITH ARUGULA PESTO AND SALMON

PREPARATION: 35 minutes
COOKING TIME: 40 minutes
DIFFICULTY: MEDIUM

4 SERVINGS

12 oz. (350 g) Barilla sedanini rigati
3 1/2 oz. (100 g) arugula
1 cup (200 ml) extra-virgin olive oil
3/4 oz. (20 g) pine nuts
1 3/4 oz. (50 g) potatoes
1/4 cup (50 ml) vegetable broth
7 oz. (200 g) fresh salmon, cut into cubes
3/4 oz. (20 g) shallots, peeled
4 oz. (120 g) cherry tomatoes, quartered
1 clove garlic
1 tsp. chopped fresh rosemary
1 tsp. (5 ml) vodka

Scrub the potatoes. Cook them in salted boiling water, skins on, until tender, about 15 minutes.

Drain and peel the potatoes. In a blender, blend the potatoes with 3/4 cup (150 ml) of the olive oil and the arugula, whole garlic clove, pine nuts, and vegetable broth.

Heat the remaining 1/4 cup of oil in a large pan and sauté the chopped shallots, then add the salmon. Season with salt and pepper, then add the vodka and allow it to evaporate. Add the quartered tomatoes and chopped rosemary, and cook for 4 to 5 minutes. When they are cooked, mix the contents of both pans together.

Meanwhile, bring a large pot of salted water to a boil and cook the sedanini rigati until it is al dente; drain. Toss pasta with the sauce to combine and serve.

ALTERNATIVE VERSIONS
Short pastas go perfectly with this sauce. Instead of sedanini rigati, you could try penne rigate, fusilli, or pipe rigate.

I ♥ Pasta

MARGHERITA SALAD WITH SEDANINI RIGATI

PREPARATION: 15 minutes
COOKING TIME: 12 minutes
DIFFICULTY: EASY

4 SERVINGS

12 oz. (350 g) Barilla sedanini rigati
9 oz. (250 g) cherry tomatoes
7 oz. (200 g) mozzarella
1/3 cup (80 ml) extra-virgin olive oil
4-5 fresh basil leaves, hand-torn
Oregano (fresh or dried) to taste,
for garnish
Salt to taste

Bring a pot of salted water to a boil and cook the sedanini rigati until just al dente. Drain and rinse with cold running water.

Transfer to a large bowl and toss with a drizzle of olive oil so that the pasta does not stick together.

Cut the cherry tomatoes and mozzarella into a medium dice. Combine both with the pasta.

Toss with a pinch of salt, the basil, and the oil and serve. Garnish with oregano to taste.

ALTERNATIVE VERSIONS
This Margherita Salad can be used with other short pasta shapes, such as farfalle, cellentani, and pipe rigate.

I ♥ Pasta

TORTIGLIONI
WITH PARMIGIANO REGGIANO FONDUE
AND BALSAMIC VINEGAR

PREPARATION TIME: 12 minutes
COOKING TIME: 12 minutes
DIFFICULTY: EASY

4 SERVINGS

12 oz. (350 g) Barilla tortiglioni
1 1/4 cups (300 ml) heavy cream
1 1/4 cups (120 g) grated
Parmigiano Reggiano cheese
Balsamic vinegar, preferably
of Modena; as needed
Salt and pepper to taste

Bring a pot of salted water to a boil for the pasta.

Meanwhile, in a large pan over low heat, bring the heavy cream to a simmer. Add the Parmigiano Reggiano and mix well to obtain a smooth fondue. Season with salt and pepper, and keep warm.

Cook the tortiglioni in the pot of boiling salted water until it is al dente; drain. Transfer the pasta to the pan with the Parmigiano Reggiano fondue and mix well. Serve, drizzling it with a few drops of balsamic vinegar.

ALTERNATIVE VERSIONS
This recipe pairs well with short pasta. Instead of tortiglioni, you can use farfalle, mezze penne rigate, and conchiglie rigate.

WHOLE-GRAIN TORTIGLIONI WITH PEPPERS

PREPARATION: 20 minutes
COOKING TIME: 20 minutes
DIFFICULTY: EASY

4 SERVINGS

12 oz. (350 g) Barilla whole-grain tortiglioni
1/4 cup (50 ml) extra-virgin olive oil
1 red bell pepper, cored, seeded, and finely sliced
1 yellow bell pepper, cored, seeded, and finely sliced
3 1/2 oz. (100 g) onion, peeled and sliced
1/2 cup (100 ml) heavy cream
Salt and pepper to taste

Heat the oil in a pan and sauté the onion. Add the peppers and cook until soft, adding a little water if necessary.

Season with salt and pepper. When the pepper sauce is cooked, blend in the heavy cream.

Bring a large pot of salted water to a boil and cook the whole-grain tortiglioni until it is al dente; drain.

Toss pasta with the sauce to combine and serve.

ALTERNATIVE VERSIONS
This recipe is also excellent with other pastas, such as whole-grain cellentani, rigatoni, and pipe rigate.

I ♥ Pasta

LIGURIAN TROFIE WITH GENOA-STYLE PESTO

PREPARATION: 15 minutes
COOKING TIME: 10 minutes
DIFFICULTY: EASY

4 SERVINGS

12 oz. (350 g) Barilla Ligurian trofie
1 oz. (30 g) fresh basil leaves
1/2 cup plus 2 tbsp. (60 g) grated Parmigiano Reggiano cheese
1/3 cup plus 1 1/2 tbsp. (40 g) grated aged Pecorino cheese
1/4 oz. (10 g) pine nuts, or about 1 tbsp.
3/4 cup plus 2 tbsp. (200 ml) extra-virgin olive oil, preferably from Liguria
3 1/2 oz. (100 g) green beans, chopped
7 oz. (200 g) potatoes, peeled and diced
1 clove garlic
Salt

Rinse and thoroughly dry the basil.

To make the pesto sauce, use a blender or food processor to pulse the basil with 2/3 cup (150 ml) of olive oil, a pinch of salt, the garlic, and the pine nuts until well combined. Add both cheeses and pulse to combine.

Transfer pesto to a large bowl, drizzle remaining oil over the top, and set aside.

Bring a pot of salted water to a boil and cook the green beans, the potatoes, and the trofie together until the pasta is al dente. Drain (reserving a little of the pasta water) and place in a bowl with the pesto. Toss to combine, diluting with a bit of the pasta water and a drizzle of olive oil if pesto is too thick.

ALTERNATIVE VERSIONS
This classic regional recipe can also be prepared with bavette.

LIGURIAN TROFIE WITH WALNUT SAUCE

PREPARATION: 15 minutes
COOKING TIME: 10 minutes
DIFFICULTY: EASY

4 SERVINGS

12 oz. (350 g) Barilla Ligurian trofie
1 3/4 oz. (50 g) shelled walnuts
1/2 oz. (15 g) pine nuts
1 oz. (25 g) day-old white bread, or
about 1 slice
½ cup (100 ml) milk; plus more
if needed
½ cup (100 ml) extra-virgin olive
oil, preferably from Liguria
1/4 cup (20 g) grated
Parmigiano Reggiano cheese
1 clove garlic
1 tsp. marjoram leaves (optional)
Salt to taste

Soak the walnuts in boiling water for a few minutes, to remove their skins. Slice off and discard bread crusts, soak the crustless bread in milk, then squeeze out excess.

Place all the ingredients in a blender and blend until the sauce is smooth, adding a little more milk if necessary.

Bring a pot of salted water to a boil and cook the Ligurian trofie until it is al dente. Drain, but reserve some of the cooking water.

Toss trofie with the walnut sauce, diluting with a little of the cooking water, if necessary. Garnish with a few leaves of marjoram.

ALTERNATIVE VERSIONS
This classic regional recipe can also be prepared with bavette.

BAKED AND EGG PASTA

THE UTMOST IN DELICIOUSNESS

I ♥ Pasta

Golden and fragrant egg pasta offers the height of goodness and is, without doubt, the most appetizing pasta of all. Originating as a traditional pasta, handmade and rolled by the women of Emilia-Romagna, it comes in a variety of shapes. There are long shapes, such as the classic tagliatelle—traditionally prepared with a rich and tasty Bolognese sauce—or fettuccine, delicious simply with fresh butter and Parmigiano Reggiano cheese or with a porcini mushroom sauce. There are the short pastas, such as maltagliati—with their irregular shape, thickness, and size, originally made using the scraps of dough that were left over from preparing tagliatelle or stuffed pasta—or garganelli, squares of dough rolled up on themselves, with pointed, slanted tips. There are baked pastas like lasagna—popular from as far back as Roman times, when it used to be cooked with layers of legumes and cheese, and now prepared with a variety of meat, fish, or vegetable sauces, or with pesto—and cannelloni, to be stuffed with equally varied fillings. And then there are the small soup shapes, such as grattini, which we suggest serving with an inviting fish broth.

With its rough and porous texture, egg pasta absorbs every sauce to perfection, enriching any recipe with flavor and aroma. Each pasta shape, however, requires the right sauce pairing. Green-hued egg lasagna (its color comes from adding spinach to the dough) is perfect with a Bolognese. In terms of stuffed pasta, tortellini with Parma ham are excellent in stock or seasoned with a delicate, creamy pea sauce, while tortelloni stuffed with ricotta and spinach are best served simply with melted butter and sage.

Given this type of pasta's long and glorious past, it features considerably in the gastronomic culture of northern Italy: for example, egg tagliolini Monferrina-style, seasoned with butter infused with herbs and garlic, and topped with a generous sprinkling of Parmigiano Reggiano cheese, or spaghetti alla chitarra, Gricia-style, typical of Lazio, flavored with guanciale or bacon and chile-pepper sauce, plus a sprinkling of grated Pecorino Romano.

EGG CANNELLONI

STUFFED WITH VEGETABLES, RICOTTA AND OTHER CHEESES, AND TOPPED WITH RICH MEAT SAUCES,
THEN BAKED AU GRATIN WITH BÉCHAMEL.

Central Italy, and now widespread throughout Italy.

The name derives from the Italian term *canna* ("pipe"), and, more specifically, *cannello*, used to indicate a short tube. *Cannelloni* are also called *cannacciotti* or *canneroni*, as well as *Manfrigoli* in Valtellina, *cannaroni* in the area of Naples (a term referring to the shape of the esophagus of animals), *schiaffettoni* in Calabria, and *cannoli* or *crusetti* in Sicily.

Cannelloni *are a relatively young pasta variety. The earliest records date back to the mid-nineteenth century in the recipe book handwritten by the cook Gio Batta Magi (1842–1885) from Arezzo, who describes the preparation of a macaroni pie. This is perhaps a smaller version of the "stuffed macaroni" previously mentioned by Vincenzo Corrado in* Il cuoco galante, *published in Naples in 1773. However, it is only in twentieth-century cookbooks that cannelloni make their appearance in their own right, prepared with a meat filling and cooked au gratin with béchamel. Legend has it, as related by Gaetano Afeltra, that their invention in 1924 by Salvatore Coletta, the chef of the restaurant at the Hotel Cappuccini in Amalfi, was heralded by the ringing of church bells. Since then, it has been considered the festive dish.*

≪*At 1 o'clock in the afternoon on a blazing hot August day in 1924, when the whole town seemed to be numbed by a shower of dazzling light that the reflection of the sea turned into a vanishing mist, suddenly the church bells of the monastery founded by St. Francis in 1222 began to ring a full peal, as it does on Easter day, at the time of the Resurrection. Amalfi was suddenly awakened from its slumber. What good news did that gay sound carry?*
All the people of the town asked themselves that very question as they craned their necks from the balconies, but no one could find an answer. Only the Capuchins in the old monastery knew.
In Amalfi, relations between the two hotels—the Hotel Luna and the Hotel Cappuccini—were based on mutual respect and chivalrous loyalty. Both hotel 'dynasties'—the Barbaros from the Luna and the Vozzis from the Cappuccini—had adhered strictly to a rule that nei-

ther had ever broken. When the kitchen of one of the two hotels invented a new dish, the other was entitled to the first taste and judgment. And so it happened on that day in August of 1924. The Chef Salvatore Coletta, after several highly secret experiments, had prepared a dish that he had presented personally to Don Alfredo. He had been working on it for months, and had even given it a name: cannelloni. Lined up in a dish, they featured vibrant colors and gave off a sublime scent. Don Alfredo tasted one, opened his eyes wide, and said: 'Well done Salvatore, to me this is divine. But we must seek the opinion of the Hotel Luna. Send them at once to Don Andrea Barbaro.' The messenger set off at a sprint.
Don Andrea, commonly referred to as 'the master of the Luna,' was a renowned gourmet weighing 290 pounds. He ate the entire dish voraciously and then stood up, his napkin still pinned to his neck, and gave orders to ring the bells of the convent. He believed the invention of cannelloni was an extraordinary event to be celebrated, a great culinary achievement worthy of being communicated to the people.... The bell-ringing suddenly came to the ears of the 'Cappuccini.' Don Alfredo noticed a strange fluttering on the terrace of the Hotel Luna. He looked through his binoculars: it was all the staff of the 'Luna' who was engaged in a celebratory waving of napkins: the honors of war to the winning opponent. Meanwhile, all the bells of Amalfi kept ringing.
The invention of cannelloni is without doubt the second reason of pride for the city, after that of the compass. The dish is eaten in London, in New York, and the world over; but few, even in Italy, know their real story. Salvatore Coletta will remain forever an unknown gentleman who is no more. God rest his soul.≫
From: Afeltra, Gaetano, *Nascita dei cannelloni ad Amalfi*, Cava dei Tirreni (I), Avagliano, 1987.

SHORT, HOLLOW DURUM WHEAT PASTA
Average size:
length 100.00 mm • diameter 36.00 mm • thickness 1.10 mm

EGG LASAGNA /
GREEN EGG LASAGNA

SERVED DRY, OVEN-BAKED, WITH SUMPTUOUS MEAT
OR VEGETABLE SAUCES ALTERNATED WITH BÉCHAMEL.

All regions of Italy.

Their name probably derives from the spoken Latin term *lasànum*, taken from the Greek *làsanon*, a tripod used to support pots over a fire. *Lasànea* was probably a term referring to what was cooked in the pot. Strips of pasta named *lagana* are cited in the works by the Roman philosopher Cicero, who was especially fond of them, although at that time they were probably fried rather than boiled. This name has remained in use in Puglia to this day. Over time, the name has been used for different types of pasta, even with different cooking methods. Today, it indicates wide strips of oven-baked pasta. In Veneto, it is called *bardele* or *lasagnoni*, in Liguria *cappellasci*, and in Puglia, as mentioned above, it is referred to by the name of *lagana*. There is also an industrial version with curled edges.

This is one of the oldest Italian pastas, consisting of a sheet of dough cut into different shapes and proportions from region to region. There are many records of its use in Roman times, in the Middle Ages, and during the Renaissance. Salimbene of Parma, in his thirteenth-century Chronicle, *describes the preparation of* lagana cum caseo—*namely, Lasagna with Parmesan cheese. Moreover, the fourteenth-century* Liber de coquina *includes a precise description in the Latin language of its preparation, identical to the one in use to this day. Over the centuries, local customs have varied, with regard to the type of dough—which can include spelt, rye, or chestnut flour, and, from the seventeenth-century, also corn flour,*

but also ingredients such as saffron, Swiss chard, or spinach—and in terms of the accompaniments with which it is served: meat or vegetable ragùs, interspersed with local cheeses and "balsamella" (or béchamel) sauce, as it is referred to by the Italian cookbook author Artusi in the late nineteenth century. Due to the richness of its ingredients, lasagna was once reserved for feast days, especially in southern Italy. Francis II of the Two Sicilies, the last King of Naples, was nicknamed "Lasa," short for lasagna, by his family, due to his passion for this dish. The most famous were certainly lasagna bolognese, drawing on an age-old tradition in egg pastry.

In 1935, the journalist and cooking expert Paolo Bonelli (1891-1984) thus described the legendary lasagna bolognese:

«*I have read holy, fragrant books; I have sought certainties and consolations in a thousand volumes; but no book is worth this volume of green lasagna served up by the appetite-whetting innkeepers of Bologna. Between each page is a sprinkling of cheese, a dotting of truffles, a swarming of delicious giblets. Leaf through and devour the pages: it is a miniature Decameron, a manual of Stoic philosophy, a comforting poem that makes you feel glad to be alive. Its pages conceal invisible sheet music by Rossini...*»
From: Monelli, Paolo, *Il Ghiottone errante*, Milan, Treves, 1935, p. 90.

LONG DURUM WHEAT PASTA, WITH OR WITHOUT EGG, MADE
FROM SHEETS OF DOUGH CUT WITHOUT THE USE OF DIES
Average size:
width 90.00 mm • length 170.00 mm • thickness 1.15 mm

EGG FETTUCCINE / EGG FETTUCCINE RICCE

DRY, WITH MEAT, VEGETABLE, CHEESE AND CREAM SAUCES.

Most popular in central and southern Italy, particularly in Lazio, where numerous recipes are based on this type of pasta.

The name derives from the Italian word *fettuccia*, or "ribbon." They are often confused with *tagliatelle*, *taglierini* and *tagliolini*. Fettuccine ricce (meaning curled) feature a wavy edge on one or both sides. This variety is often known as *reginette*, meaning "little queens" (probably referencing the scallops on the top of a crown), or *mafaldine*, named after the Italian Princess Mafalda of Savoy (1902–1944), daughter of Victor Emmanuel III.

Fettuccine *were considered a propitiatory food, served at weddings in many regions of central and southern Italy to ensure fertility. In Umbria, where they are called* macaroni, *they are the typical dish served on Christmas Eve, flavored with honey and nuts. In Orvieto, they were a peasant dish consumed at the time of threshing, seasoned with a goose sauce. In Abruzzo, their traditional condiment was a sauce prepared with chopped fried pickles. In Sardinia, special fettuccine known as* busaki *were traditionally served at Easter.*

Paolo Monelli describes Alfredo, the "King of Fettuccine" in Rome: ≪ *The innkeeper appeared, with a mustachioed upper lip and a tamer's tummy, clutching some golden cutlery. He approached the plate of fettuccine. The music stopped, and a rolling of drums made the customers fall silent. The innkeeper could feel everyone's eyes on him. He raised his fork and spoon up to the sky, as if to gain its favor, and then plunged them into the pasta, stirring it up with quick movements of mathematical precision, his head tilted to one side, his breath held, his little finger suspended. The silence hung heavily in the room. Then, suddenly, the music burst into cheerful play, as the innkeeper dished out the portions, before putting down his golden cutlery and disappearing.* ≫
From: Monelli, Paolo, *Il Ghiottone errante*, Milan (I), Treves, 1935, pp. 128-130.

LONG, RIBBON-SHAPED DURUM WHEAT EGG PASTA
Average size:
length 7.00 mm • thickness 0.90 mm

EGG GARGANELLI

DRY, SERVED WITH MEAT OR TOMATO AND VEGETABLE SAUCES, WITH CREAM, OR WITH BUTTER AND CHEESE.

Mainly Emilia-Romagna, but also Marche and Umbria. It is a typical specialty of Lugo, in Emilia-Romagna.

Garganelli, originating in Emilia-Romagna, have a shape that supposedly resembles the esophagus of a chicken, called *garganél* in the local dialect. They are produced using a tool called a *comb*—similar to a heddle, the instrument once used to weave fabric—consisting of two parallel slats held together by strips of cane. The square of dough is placed sideways on the comb, and, with the aid of a stick, is wrapped over itself, thus forming a tube with pointed ends. The outside, which rests on the comb, takes on small ridges and a striped appearance.

In Emilia-Romagna, garganelli *were once traditionally served in capon stock, and the dough was enriched with nutmeg and grated cheese. Legend has it that we owe the birth of this characteristic shape...to a cat! After a housewife had prepared the meat filling for tortellini, her feline devoured it. The woman, having already*

cut the dough into squares, and not wanting to send her guests away with empty stomachs, is said to have wrapped the squares around a stick and rubbed the loom comb over them, thus salvaging her lunch with creativity and intelligence. A similar technique is used in the nearby Marche, in Sassoferrato, to produce macaroni con le battecche, *formed by rolling a strip of long pasta into a spiral around a willow stick and streaking it with a comb.*

DURUM WHEAT EGG PASTA MADE FROM CUT AND ROLLED DOUGH, WITHOUT THE USE OF DIES
Average size:
length 36.00 mm • thickness 0.90 mm

EGG GRATTINI

IT IS WIDELY SERVED IN MEAT STOCK.
IN BASILICATA, IT IS ALSO USED
FOR BEAN SOUP.

All regions of Italy.

The name, which derives from the Italian verb *grattare*, or "to scratch," indicates an irregular, grainy pasta obtained by rubbing the dough over a grater. Their names change in different regions of Italy: *pasta grattada* in Friuli, *pasta rasa* in Lombardy and Emilia (where they are also known as *grattini* or *gratèin*), *grandinina* in Tuscany (from grandine, or "hailstones"), *mollichelle* (from *mollica*, or "breadcrumbs") in Umbria, *granitte*, from the verb *granire* ("to mill") in Abruzzo and Molise, and the dialect term *mblband* (*bilbanti* in Italian, i.e. "shavings") in Basilicata.

This is the pasta shape that, in terms of texture, most closely resembles Arabic couscous, and is widely used in the Italian islands close to Africa. Indeed, the typical flour-based recipes on which Italian pasta is based first came from North Africa and the Middle East. This "grated pasta" was an easier way to achieve the popular texture of the Maghreb couscous, and soon spread across Italy. It appeared in soups, and came to be considered an invigorating way of beginning important lunches or meals served on festive occasions such as weddings. This hearty soup was also administered to new mothers as a tonic after the pains of childbirth.

Among the earlier papers of the historian Ludovico Antonio Muratori (1672–1750) is a collection of *Latin Odes*, including one dedicated to flour: ≪*Cooks rejoice at the abundance of flour-based foods, and the table is enriched, now with lasagna, and now with tagliatelle and long pasta; it is enhanced, now with gnocchi, now with grated pasta. And then, such a variety of vermicelli dishes! These are sometimes thick, and sometimes very thin.*≫
From: Sada, Luigi, *Spaghetti e Compagni*. Edizioni del Centro Librario, Biblioteca de "La Taberna". Bari (I), 1982, pp. 45-46.

**GRATED DURUM WHEAT EGG PASTA,
OBTAINED WITHOUT THE USE OF DIES**
Average size:
diameter of approximately 2.50–3.00 mm

MALTAGLIATI

USED BOTH IN SOUPS AND DRY. IN VENETO IT
IS USED FOR *PASTA E FAGIOLI* ("PASTA WITH
BEANS"), IN EMILIA IT IS FRIED WITH LARD,
AND IN THE MARCHE IT IS SERVED WITH
DUCK SAUCE. IDEAL FOR THICKENED SOUPS.

All over Italy, but traditionally mainly Lombardy, Veneto, Emilia-Romagna, Marche, and Puglia.

The name clearly indicates the preparation method, with *mal tagliato* meaning "cut badly": the dough is rolled out and shredded diagonally with a knife, to obtain irregular diamonds. *Maltagliati* is also known as *malmaritati*, and by a variety of other names in the various dialects of Italy.

When homemade, this irregular diamond-shaped pasta is traditionally obtained from the dough left over after preparing tagliatelle. The larger version earned itself the nickname of spruzzamusi, *or "face splasher": when served in stock and gobbled up greedily, the diner is at risk of splashing his face. Maltagliati can be dressed in either simple or rich sauces. It is prevalent in northern Italian regional cuisines, and in Puglia, where it is accompanied by chickpeas. It is most often used in soups—served with legumes, vegetables, or simple meat stock—but is also served dry, with meat or sausage sauces.*

DURUM WHEAT EGG PASTA MADE FROM SHEETS OF DOUGH CUT WITHOUT THE USE OF DIES
Average size:
ength 32.00 mm • thickness 1.15 mm

EGG PAGLIA E FIENO /
EGG TAGLIATELLE / EGG TAGLIOLINI

DRY, WITH MEAT, VEGETABLE, CHEESE, AND CREAM SAUCES. THE THINNER VARIETIES ARE GENERALLY COOKED IN STOCK.
PAGLIA E FIENO GOES PARTICULARLY WELL WITH BUTTER, CHEESE, AND CREAM SAUCES.

All regions of Italy.

Tagliatelle, from the verb *tagliare*, or "to cut," are one of the most typical examples of Italian pasta. They are the direct descendants of lasagna, and were originally obtained by cutting a sheet of rolled dough into regular strips, using a flat-bladed knife. They share the same etymological root with the smaller *taglierini* and *tagliolini*. They are also called *bardele* in Lombardy and *fettuccine* in Lazio. Here, the finest version takes the curious name of *sciacquabaffi*, or "mustache rinser," due to its traditional use in broth. When industrially produced, they generally come in nests or skeins. In the *paglia e fieno* ("straw and hay") variety, *tagliatelle* made with eggs (straw) are cooked together with other *tagliatelle*, whose dough has been kneaded with the addition of spinach (which is green, like hay).

Egg tagliatelle *are used in a variety of ways, from baking them in pies to boiling them in stock. This rich pasta is often considered a festive dish, and was once the pride of the good homemaker, who would learn from childhood the art of rolling the dough by hand and cutting it to size with a simple knife.*
Augusto Majani, a humorist, designer, and writer from Bologna (and better known by the pseudonym Nasica), fueled his heated debate with Filippo Tommaso Marinetti (1876–1944), the leader of the Futurist movement and an inveterate hater of dry pasta, by inventing a fictitious commemoration of the birth of tagliatelle, *supposedly created by a certain Master Zefirino, a talented court chef of the Middle Ages. The story that Master Zefirino was inspired by Lucrezia Borgia's blond hair on the occasion of her marriage to Alfonso d'Este was taken as likely by many.*
Although Bologna laid first claim to the birth of tagliatelle, *the pasta is widespread in Italy, with different names and thicknesses and sometimes with the addition of typical local ingredients, such as corn flour, vegetables such as borage or spinach, various spices,* saffron, chestnut flour, and on and on. Equally varied are the condiments, which range from delicate broths and simple butter and Parmigiano Reggiano cheese sauces, to meat ragùs and vegetable, mushroom, truffle, or walnut sauces.

A definition of tagliatelle
Giacinto Carena, in his *Vocabolario domestico* (Home Vocabulary) published in Naples in 1859, describes the preparation of tagliatelle as follows:

≪*Soak some flour in very little water, making sure this is not too cold, and break in the eggs, then mix the dough on a cutting board or on the upside-down lid of the kneading trough. The dough, once mixed, kneaded, and floured, is flattened and rolled out using a rolling pin or pastry board, reducing it to a wide sheet of pastry; this is then rolled on itself and cut crosswise into strips with a knife.*≫
From: Carena, Giacinto, *Vocabolario domestico*, Naples (I), 1859.

**LONG DURUM WHEAT EGG PASTA, ROLLED AND CUT
WITHOUT THE USE OF DIES**
Average size by *tagliatelle*:
**strip width 4.85 mm • nest diameter 55.00
• thickness 0.90 mm**
Average size by *tagliolini*:
**strip width 1.00 mm • nest diameter 55.00
• thickness 0.90 mm**
Average size by *paglia e fieno*:
**strip width 4.85 mm • nest diameter 55.00
• thickness 0.90 mm**

EGG PAPPARDELLE

DRY, WITH RICH MEAT, FOWL, AND GAME SAUCES.

Northern and central Italy, and particularly Emilia-Romagna, Marche, Umbria, Tuscany, and Abruzzo. The industrial version is widespread throughout Italy.

The term comes from the Italian terms *pappa*, a children's word for "food," and *pappare*, meaning "to gobble."

The term comes from a Tuscan term and, indeed, these wide tagliatelle are particularly popular in Tuscany, served with the many game-based sauces typical of the local cuisine. In the neighboring areas of Emilia-Romagna, Marche, Montefeltro, Umbria, and Lazio, the classic condiments that accompany this pasta dish are often based on uncommon meats, such as hare, quail, wild boar, pigeon, or duck.

In his *Secchia rapita*, the poet Alessandro Tassoni, from Modena (1565–1635), refers to one of the fallen of the war of 1325 as:

《*... the miser Baccarin, his banner furled,*
Inventor of pappardelle and lectuary,
Was left defunct, with others, also slain,
To fatten with their limbs Rubiera's plain.》

From: Tassoni, Alessandro, *La secchia rapita*, Paris (F), 1622, Canto IV, 30-35.

DURUM WHEAT PASTA MADE FROM A SHEET OF DOUGH WRAPPED INTO THE SHAPE OF A NEST, WITHOUT THE USE OF DIES
Average size:
length 18.00 mm • thickness 0.90 mm

PARMA HAM TORTELLINI
RICOTTA-AND-SPINACH TORTELLONI

IN MEAT STOCK, OR DRY WITH MEAT OR CREAM AND CHEESE SAUCES.

Emilia-Romagna, Bologna, and Modena in particular, and as an industrial production, all regions of Italy.

Small or large *tortelli*, from the diminutive or augmentative form of the Italian word *torta*, or cake, used to indicate a round dessert. The term, borrowed from baking and altered in meaning, suggests the presence of a filling.

This stuffed pasta is typical of Emilia, and more particularly of Modena and Bologna. Stuffed pasta was born both in the elaborate and rich recipes of the cooks at court and in family kitchens. It spread, with endless variations, across Emilia-Romagna: tortellini, tortelletti, tortelloni, anolini, and cappelletti generally indicate completely different products, both in terms of shape and stuffing. Traditionally, these stuffed pastas are almost always cooked in stock prepared with various meats. However, they can also be served dry, with rich sauces and cream, or with unusual meats, such as pigeon, in pastry pies. Moreover, special sweet and savory

recipes refer back to the unusual flavor combinations used in the kitchens of the Renaissance courts. Tortelloni with ricotta and spinach, typical of Parma, are traditionally prepared dry, with butter and cheese. In Parma and in Emilia, on the evening of St. John, they are served outdoors on long tables that gather together the inhabitants of entire streets and villages.

STUFFED DURUM WHEAT PASTA
Average size by *tortellini*:
diameter 21.00 mm • sheet thickness 0.90 mm
Average size by *tortelloni*:
length 45.00 mm • sheet thickness 1.15 mm

SPAGHETTI ALLA CHITARRA

DRY, WITH MEAT OR VEGETABLE SAUCES AND WITH LAMB *RAGÙ*.

Traditionally Abruzzo and Molise, but today all regions of Italy.

This pasta is cut using a special tool, called a *chitarra*, or "guitar," a wooden frame on which numerous parallel steel wires are tied. The tool's shape and taut wires make it similar in appearance to the musical instrument for which it's named. The dough is rolled out to a moderate thinness (the same thickness as that between each wire of the *chitarra*), and is rested on the wires, where it is cut into shape by pressing on it with a special short rolling pin. The square-shaped *spaghetti* are then collected in a container beneath the guitar.

This long, square-sectioned pasta made with egg is typical of Abruzzo and Molise, where it is produced using the tool known as a chitarra, or "guitar." The distance between the cords varies according to the pasta variety required: when the cords are close together, the pasta is known as spaghetti tutt'ova, *and is as thin as* capelli d'angelo; *the thickest, or* spaghetti mezz'ovo, *is obtained by setting the cords farther apart. The* guitar *used to make this kind of pasta was once produced exclusively by the artisans of Secinaro and Pretoro, two small centers located in the current provinces of L'Aquila and Chieti. Spaghetti alla Chitarra, also called* tonarelli, *are closely linked with the cuisine of Abruzzo and Molise, and are sold both fresh and dried.*

≪ *The Genoese* fidelli *and the Italian* fidelini *are reflected in the Sardinian* findeos, *the Catalan* fideus, *the Castilian* fideos *(the latter widespread in South America, as well as in Spain), and the modern* fides. *This is a term that has spread across the Mediterranean, perhaps due to the use of a common instrument to produce long shapes of pasta. It probably derives from the Latin word* fides, *or cord, also adopted, on the basis of the concept of synecdoche—the term for a part of something being used to refer to the whole—for the cords as a whole, i.e. a lyre or a harp. These instruments were laid on the table and covered with a layer of dough. This, once rolled over with a rolling pin, would cut up into square spaghetti. This system is still in use today with the guitar from Abruzzo.* ≫
From: Agnesi, Vincenzo, *Alcune notizie sugli spaghetti*, Imperia (I), p.m., 1975, p. 91.

LONG DURUM-WHEAT EGG PASTA
Average size:
length 255.00 mm • thickness 1.70 mm

EGG CANNELLONI WITH ASPARAGUS AND BACCALÀ

PREPARATION: 45 minutes
COOKING TIME: 45 minutes
DIFFICULTY: MEDIUM

4 SERVINGS

12 Barilla oven-ready egg cannelloni

For the filling
1 oz. (30 g) shallots, or about 1 medium shallot, peeled and chopped
14 oz. (400 g) asparagus
8 3/4 oz. (250 g) baccalà (salt cod), soaked and cut into large dice
1/3 cup (30 g) grated Parmigiano Reggiano cheese
3 tbsp. (40 ml) extra-virgin olive oil
1/4 cup (50 ml) vegetable broth
1 clove garlic
Salt and pepper to taste

For the béchamel
2 cups (1/2 l) milk
1 oz. (25 g) unsalted butter
2 tbsp. (20 g) all-purpose flour
Salt to taste

For the béchamel, melt the butter in a heavy-bottomed pan. To make a roux, add the flour and whisk butter and flour together for 3 to 4 minutes over low heat, until smooth.

Heat the milk in a separate pan, then add to the roux, pouring it in a slow stream. Adjust the salt and continue cooking, whisking constantly to avoid the formation of lumps, until the sauce is thick and creamy. If the béchamel is too thick, add a bit of milk. If it is too thin, let it cook for a few additional minutes.

Remove the tough bottom ends of the asparagus stalks and discard, then thinly slice stalks. Heat the oil in a medium pan and sauté the chopped shallots with the whole garlic clove. Add asparagus and sauté until lightly browned. Add the baccalà and season with salt and pepper. Add the broth, bring to a boil, and cook filling for about 10 minutes. Let cool, add the grated Parmigiano Reggiano, then stir to combine.

Heat the oven to 350°F (180°C). Use a pastry bag to fill the cannelloni, or spoon the filling in, dividing evenly. Butter a 9-by-13-inch baking dish and arrange the filled cannelloni evenly in pan. Finish with a uniform layer of béchamel. Cover with aluminum foil and bake for 10 minutes. Uncover and bake 10 minutes more. Let the cannelloni rest for 5 minutes before serving.

I ♥ Pasta

EGG CANNELLONI AU GRATIN

PREPARATION: 45 minutes
COOKING TIME: 50 minutes
DIFFICULTY: MEDIUM

4 SERVINGS

12 Barilla oven-ready egg cannelloni
2 3/4 oz. (80 g) unsalted butter, cut
into pieces

For the filling
9 oz. (250 g) ground beef
7 oz. (200 g) cooked spinach
4 1/2 tbsp. (60 ml) dry white wine
2 tbsp. (40 ml) extra-virgin olive oil
1 1/2 oz. (40 g) onion
1 oz. (30 g) carrot
3/4 oz. (20 g) celery
1 1/3 cups (120 g) grated
Parmigiano Reggiano cheese
1 large egg
Grated nutmeg to taste
Salt and pepper to taste

For the béchamel
2 cups (500 ml) milk
1 oz. (25 g) unsalted butter
2 tbsp. (20 g) all-purpose flour
Grated nutmeg to taste
Salt to taste

For the filling, chop the onion, carrot, and celery. Heat the oil in a skillet over medium heat and sauté the vegetables until lightly browned. Add the ground beef and brown. Add the white wine, raise the heat to high, and cook until wine is completely evaporated. Add the spinach, season with a pinch of salt and a dash of pepper, and continue cooking the mixture over medium heat for 15 to 20 minutes.

Remove from heat and let the mixture cool to room temperature. Transfer to a food processor and pulse mixture. Add the egg, half of the grated Parmigiano Reggiano, and a pinch of nutmeg and pulse until thoroughly combined.

For the béchamel, melt the butter in a heavy-bottomed pan. To make a roux, add the flour and whisk butter and flour together for 3 to 4 minutes over low heat, until smooth.

Heat the milk in a separate pan, then add to the roux, pouring it in a slow stream. Adjust the salt, season with a bit of nutmeg, and continue cooking, whisking constantly to avoid the formation of lumps, until the sauce is thick and creamy. If the béchamel is too thick, add a bit of milk. If it is too thin, let it cook for a few additional minutes.

Heat the oven to 375°F (190°C). Use a pastry bag to fill the cannelloni. Butter a 9-by-13-inch baking dish and arrange the filled cannelloni evenly in pan. Finish with a uniform layer of béchamel, dusting it with the remaining cheese, and dotting the top with the pieces of butter. Bake the cannelloni for 15 to 20 minutes, until lightly browned. Remove them from the oven and let them rest for several minutes before serving.

I ♥ Pasta

EGG FETTUCCINE ALLA CACCIATORA

PREPARATION: 30 minutes
COOKING TIME: 35 minutes
DIFFICULTY: MEDIUM

4 SERVINGS

9 oz. (250 g) Barilla egg fettuccine
Half of a deboned rabbit, cut into small pieces
14 oz. (400 g) peeled tomatoes
2 oz. (60 g) pancetta, chopped
2 2/3 oz. (75 g) onion, sliced
1/4 cup (50 ml) Marsala wine
2 tbsp. (30 ml) extra-virgin olive oil
1/3 cup plus 1 1/2 tbsp. (40 g) grated Parmigiano Reggiano cheese
1 clove garlic
1 sprig rosemary
Small bunch of sage, torn
Salt and pepper to taste

In a pan over medium, heat oil and chopped pancetta. Remove rosemary needles from stem. Add the onion, the whole peeled garlic clove, the sage, and the rosemary needles and brown the mixture.

Add the rabbit and brown for several minutes.

Add the Marsala and cook until liquid evaporates, then pass the tomatoes through a vegetable mill and add them. Season with salt and pepper, reduce heat to low, and continue cooking for about 20 minutes. If the sauce becomes too dry, add a few spoonfuls of hot water. Discard the garlic clove once cooking has finished.

Bring a pot of salted water to a boil and cook the fettuccine until it is al dente; drain. Toss with the rabbit sauce and grated Parmigiano Reggiano and serve.

ALTERNATIVE VERSIONS
This sauce also pairs well with long egg pasta such as tagliatelle or pappardelle.

EGG FETTUCCINE WITH BUTTER AND PARMIGIANO REGGIANO

PREPARATION: 10 minutes
COOKING TIME: 10 minutes
DIFFICULTY: EASY

4 SERVINGS

9 oz. (250 g) Barilla egg fettuccine
6 1/2 oz. (180 g) unsalted butter
3/4 cup (80 g) grated
Parmigiano Reggiano cheese

Bring a pot of salted water to a boil and cook the egg fettuccine until al dente. Drain, reserving the cooking water.

Meanwhile, melt the butter over low heat in a pan. Toss the egg fettuccine with the melted butter and the grated Parmigiano Reggiano, stirring in up to 1 cup of cooking water. Serve hot.

ALTERNATIVE VERSIONS
This simple yet delicious recipe can be prepared using two other long egg pastas: taglierini and tagliatelle.

EGG FETTUCCINE RICCE WITH PORCINI MUSHROOMS

PREPARATION: 20 minutes
COOKING TIME: 15 minutes
DIFFICULTY: EASY

4 SERVINGS

9 oz. (250 g) Barilla egg fettuccine ricce
2 tbsp. (30 ml) extra-virgin olive oil
14 oz. (400 g) porcini mushrooms
3/4 oz. (20 g) fresh parsley, chopped
1 tbsp. (20 ml) dry white wine
1 clove garlic
Salt and pepper to taste

Scrub and slice the mushrooms.

Sauté the whole garlic clove and parsley in the oil.

Add the mushrooms and cook for about 5 minutes, making sure that the mushrooms remain firm.

Add the white wine and season with salt and pepper.

Bring a pot of salted water to a boil and cook the fettuccine until it is al dente; drain. Transfer to the pan with the mushrooms and mix well over medium heat for a few minutes.

ALTERNATIVE VERSIONS
This recipe is excellent with long egg pasta such as tagliatelle or pappardelle.

EGG FETTUCCINE RICCE WITH CABBAGE RAGÙ

PREPARATION: 45 minutes
COOKING TIME: 20 minutes
DIFFICULTY: EASY

4 SERVINGS

9 oz. (250 g) Barilla egg
fettuccine ricce
1/4 cup (50 ml) extra-virgin olive oil
3 1/2 oz. (100 g) white cabbage
3 1/2 oz. (100 g) red cabbage
6 Brussels sprouts
3 1/2 oz. (100 g) green
cauliflower florets
3 1/2 oz. (100 g) broccoli florets
1/2 cup (100 ml) white wine
1/3 cup plus 1 1/2 tbsp. (40 g) grated
Parmigiano Reggiano cheese
1 1/2 oz. (40 g) almonds, chopped
1 3/4 oz. (50 g) leeks, white and
pale green parts only
6 fresh bay leaves
Salt and pepper to taste

Wash all the vegetables. Cut the leeks and cabbage into strips and halve the Brussels sprouts.

Parboil the sprouts and the broccoli and cauliflower florets separately in salted boiling water, just until crisp-tender.

Cook the leeks in a pan with the oil and bay leaves; then add the cabbage strips, season with salt and pepper, and sauté briefly. Add the wine and let it evaporate. Add the florets and sprouts and, if necessary, a little water. Season with salt and pepper, and mix well for a few minutes over low heat.

Bring a pot of salted water to a boil and cook the fettuccine ricce until al dente; drain. Toss with the cabbage sauce. Sprinkle with the grated Parmigiano Reggiano and the chopped almonds and serve.

ALTERNATIVE VERSIONS

This cabbage sauce is excellent with other long egg pasta, such as pappardelle, tagliatelle larghe, and fettuccine.

GARGANELLI WITH PUMPKIN, PANCETTA, AND BALSAMIC VINEGAR

PREPARATION: 40 minutes
COOKING TIME: 40 minutes
DIFFICULTY: EASY

4 SERVINGS

9 oz. (250 g) Barilla garganelli
11 oz. (300 g) pumpkin
7 oz. (200 g) smoked pancetta, sliced 1/8-inch (3-mm) thick
1 1/2 tbsp. (20 ml) extra-virgin olive oil
3 cups (750 ml) water
1 yellow onion, peeled and chopped
1 tbsp. chopped parsley
1 sprig rosemary, chopped
1 clove garlic, chopped
Balsamic vinegar, preferably of Modena, to taste
Salt and pepper to taste

ALTERNATIVE VERSIONS

This sauce can also be added to non-egg pasta shapes, such as penne (lisce or rigate), mezze maniche rigate, and pipe rigate.

Cut the pumpkin in half with a serrated knife. Scrape out and discard seeds and any loose fibers from inside pumpkin.

Peel one half of the pumpkin and cut into a 1/2 inch (1 cm) dice; set aside. Cut the other half of the pumpkin into smaller sections and place in a large pot with the chopped onion and a pinch of salt. Add the 3 cups (750 ml) (or enough to cover) water, bring to a boil, and cook until tender, about 25 minutes. Drain, reserving cooking water. Let pumpkin cool, then scoop flesh from peel. Transfer cooked pumpkin and onion to a blender and purée. If mixture is too thick, add a bit of the cooking water.
Cut the pancetta into thin strips.

Heat the oil in a pan and sauté the diced pumpkin until tender. Season it with salt and pepper, remove from pan with a slotted spoon, and set aside. Sauté the pancetta in the same pan. When the fat starts to brown, add the garlic, the rosemary, and half the parsley and cook for 2 minutes. Add the pumpkin purée and diced pumpkin.

Bring a pot of salted water to a boil and cook the garganelli until al dente; drain. Toss pasta with the sauce. Stir quickly, incorporating the diced pumpkin. Top with remaining parsley and a few drops of balsamic vinegar.

EGG GRATTINI IN FISH SAUCE

PREPARATION: 45 minutes
COOKING TIME: 9 minutes
DIFFICULTY: HIGH

4 SERVINGS

7 oz. (200 g) Barilla egg grattini
7 oz. (200 g) baby octopus
14 oz. (400 g) tub gurnard or cod
4 oz. (120 g) mullet
1 3/4 oz. (50 g) squid rings
7 oz. (200 g) cuttlefish
3 1/2 oz. (100 g) mussels
3 1/2 oz. (100 g) clams
1/3 cup plus 1 1/2 tbsp. (100 ml)
extra-virgin olive oil
1 3/4 oz. (50 g) onion, peeled and
thinly sliced
4 plum tomatoes, or 12 (350 g)
canned peeled tomatoes
1 tbsp. minced fresh parsley
1 clove garlic
Salt and black pepper, or red chile
pepper, to taste
8 slices bread, toasted (optional)

Thoroughly soak and clean the clams and the mussels (and debeard the mussels. Place clams and mussels in a pan with 1 tablespoon of olive oil, the whole garlic clove, and a pinch of parsley over medium-high heat. Let the clams and mussels open (discarding any that do not open). Remove the shells. Strain the cooking juices and reserve.

Scale, gut, and fillet the tub gurnard (or cod) and the mullet, then cut them into 1-inch (2-3 cm) strips. Clean the cuttlefish, baby octopus, and squid: cut off small tentacles under eye, squeeze out and discard beak, trim off "wings." Run the dull edge of a knife down the squid to peel off membrane, and squeeze out the viscera, including the skeleton. Rinse cleaned tentacles and bodies under running water. Cut large tentacles in half, and bodies into rings or strips.

In a covered saucepan, lightly sauté onion in oil over low heat. Meanwhile, peel, seed, and dice the tomatoes, if using fresh tomatoes; add to onion when golden brown. Cook 5 minutes, then add fish. Season with salt and cook 15 to 20 minutes, diluting the sauce, if necessary, with a few ladlesful of hot water. Toward the end of the cooking time, add the mussels and clams and their juices. When the fish is ready, run it through a meat grinder, and return to pan. Add the egg grattini and cook the pasta directly in the sauce, until it is al dente. Serve the egg grattini in fish sauce piping hot, adding a sprinkling of minced parsley and freshly ground black pepper (or crumbled red chili pepper). If you wish, serve the dish with slices of toasted bread.

ALTERNATIVE VERSIONS

This fish sauce is also excellent with other soup pastas, such as risoni, tempestine, and egg risi.

EGG LASAGNA WITH RADICCHIO AND MASCARPONE

PREPARATION: 30 minutes
COOKING TIME: 45 minutes
DIFFICULTY: MEDIUM

4 SERVINGS

10 sheets Barilla oven-ready egg lasagna

For the radicchio sauce
1 lb. 2 oz. (500 g) radicchio, cut into strips
3 1/2 oz. (100 g) leeks, white parts only, thinly sliced
8 3/4 oz. (250 g) mascarpone cheese
1/2 cup (100 ml) red wine
1/3 cup (30 g) grated Parmigiano Reggiano cheese
1 1/2 oz. (40 g) unsalted butter
2 tbsp. (30 ml) extra-virgin olive oil
1 sprig thyme
1 tbsp. parsley, chopped
Salt to taste

For the béchamel
2 cups (400 ml) milk
1 oz. (25 g) unsalted butter
2 tbsp. (20 g) all-purpose flour
Salt to taste

Heat a pan with the oil over medium-low and sweat the radicchio and the leeks until softened, about 5 minutes. Add the red wine and cook over medium heat until it evaporates. Season with salt. Remove the leaves of thyme from stem and add to the mixture with the chopped parsley only after the vegetables are done cooking (after about 15 minutes).

Meanwhile, prepare the béchamel. Melt the butter in a heavy-bottomed pan. To make a roux, add the flour and whisk butter and flour together for 3 to 4 minutes over low heat, until smooth.

Heat the milk in a separate pan, then add to the roux, pouring it in a slow stream. Adjust the salt and continue cooking, whisking constantly to avoid the formation of lumps, until the sauce is thick and creamy. If the béchamel is too thick, add a bit of milk. If it is too thin, let it cook for a few additional minutes. Salt to taste, let cool, and mix in the mascarpone. Heat the oven to 340°F (170°C).

Melt half the butter and grease the bottom of a 9-by-13-inch baking dish and arrange the first layer of lasagna sheets lengthwise. Continue, alternating between the radicchio sauce and the mascarpone béchamel, always separated by a layer of pasta, until you have used all the ingredients. Cut the remaining butter into pieces and dot the top of the lasagna. Sprinkle with the grated Parmigiano Reggiano.

Cover the pan with a sheet of aluminum foil (taking care not to let it come into contact with the lasagna) and bake it for 15 minutes. Remove the foil and let it continue to cook for another 10 minutes, or until golden brown.

I ♥ Pasta

GENOA-STYLE EGG LASAGNA

PREPARATION: 35 minutes
COOKING TIME: 45 minutes
DIFFICULTY: MEDIUM

4 SERVINGS

8 sheets Barilla oven-ready egg lasagna
3 1/2 oz. (100 g) potatoes
1 3/4 oz. (50 g) green beans

For the pesto sauce
2 2/3 oz. (75 g) basil leaves, rinsed and dried
3 tbsp. (25 g) pine nuts
1/2 cup (50 g) grated Parmigiano Reggiano cheese
1/4 cup (25 g) grated Pecorino Sardo cheese
1 clove garlic
2 3/4 tbsp. (40 ml) extra-virgin olive oil

For the béchamel
2 cups (500 ml) milk
1 oz. (30 g) unsalted butter
2 tbsp. (25 g) all-purpose flour
Salt to taste

To make the pesto, put the pine nuts and the whole garlic clove into a food processor and blend the mixture. With food processor running, add the basil and the olive oil. Add the grated cheese (reserving a small amount of grated Parmigiano Reggiano for garnish), and adjust the thickness of the mixture by adding more oil, if necessary. Scrub, peel, and cube the potatoes; then rinse and cut the green beans into a large dice. Cook the potatoes and green beans together in boiling salted water until the beans are crisp-tender, about 10 minutes; drain.

For the béchamel, melt the butter in a heavy-bottomed pan. To make a roux, add the flour and whisk butter and flour together for 3 to 4 minutes over low heat, until smooth. Heat the milk in a separate pan, then add to the roux, pouring it in a slow stream. Adjust salt and continue cooking, whisking constantly, until the sauce is thick and creamy. If béchamel is too thick, add milk. If it is too thin, let it cook for a few additional minutes.

Heat oven to 350°F (180°C). Butter a medium rectangular baking dish. To make the lasagna, spread a bit of the béchamel, pesto, green beans, and potatoes on the bottom of the baking dish and cover with 2 sheets of lasagna side by side. Repeat, layering lasagna sheets and sauce, for a total of 4 layers. Cover the top layer with béchamel and the reserved Parmigiano Reggiano. Bake for 20 to 25 minutes. Let rest for 5 minutes before serving.

ALTERNATIVE VERSIONS
For a dish with richer color and a vegetable pairing, you can use spinach egg lasagna.

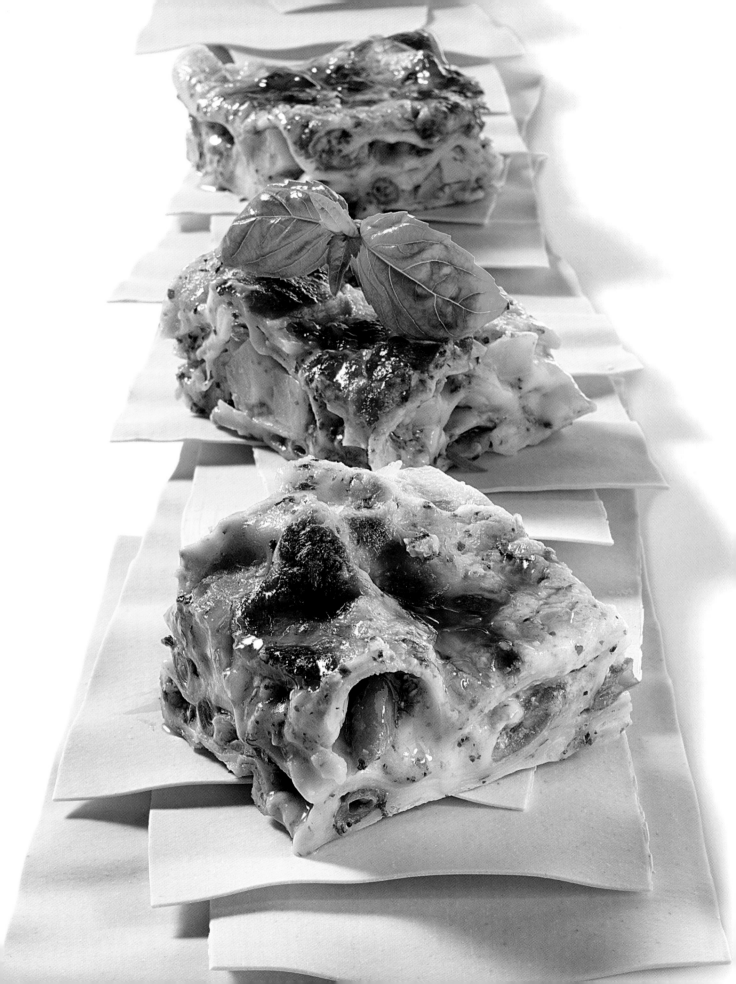

EGG LASAGNA WITH MONKFISH AND CLAMS

PREPARATION: 1 hour
COOKING TIME: 30 minutes
DIFFICULTY: HIGH

4 SERVINGS

8 sheets Barilla oven-ready egg lasagna

For the sauce
1/4 cup (50 ml) extra-virgin olive oil
12 oz. (350 g) monkfish
11 oz. (300 g) clams
1 sprig parsley, chopped
1/2 cup (100 ml) white wine
8 jumbo shrimp
4 oz. (120 g) cherry tomatoes
1 clove garlic
Crushed red chile pepper flakes to taste
Salt and black pepper to taste

For the roux
2 1/2 tbsp. unsalted butter
1/4 cup (30 g) all-purpose flour
2 cups (500 ml) fish stock
Salt to taste

ALTERNATIVE VERSIONS
This recipe can also be prepared with spinach egg lasagna.

Scrub and rinse the clams. Heat half the olive oil in a pan with the whole garlic clove, the parsley, the white wine, and chile pepper to taste. Add the clams and cook until they are open, discarding any that do not open. Once clams open, remove the shells and strain (and reserve) the liquid.

Clean and fillet the monkfish, and shell and devein the shrimp. Use the seafood scraps to prepare a fish stock.

Rinse and seed the tomatoes, then cut them into quarters. Sauté them in a hot pan with a little olive oil, and set aside.

Dice the monkfish and shrimp. Sauté them briefly in a pan, add the tomatoes, season with salt and pepper, then add the parsley and clams.

For the roux, melt the butter in a pan, making sure it does not brown. Add the flour to the butter and whisk until smooth and free of lumps. Add the fish stock and the reserved clam juices and whisk, being careful not to let lumps form. Bring to a boil and cook for 1 minute.

Heat the oven to 350°F (180°C).

Butter a 9-by-13-inch pan and line it with the roux. Place a layer of pasta over it and cover it with more roux and some fish sauce. Repeat, using all the ingredients and ending with a layer of roux and fish sauce. Bake for about 20 minutes. Let cool for 5 to 10 minutes before serving. If you wish, garnish the dish with a little roux.

SPINACH EGG LASAGNA ALLA BOLOGNESE

PREPARATION: 2 ore
COOKING TIME: 25-30 minutes
DIFFICULTY: HIGH

4 SERVINGS

8 sheets Barilla oven-ready spinach egg lasagna

For the sauce
2 tbsp. (30 ml) extra-virgin olive oil
1 oz. (30 g) celery, chopped
1 3/4 oz. (50 g) carrot, peeled and chopped
2 oz. (60 g) onion, peeled and chopped
3/4 oz. (20 g) pancetta
3 1/2 oz. (100 g) ground pork
4 oz. (120 g) ground beef
1/3 cup (80 ml) red wine
2 oz. (60 g) tomato paste
2 cups (500 ml) water
1 bay leaf
Salt and pepper to taste

For the béchamel
2 cups (500 ml) milk
1 oz. (30 g) unsalted butter
2 tbsp. (25 g) all-purpose flour
Grated nutmeg to taste
Salt to taste

For the topping
3/4 cup (80 g) grated
Parmigiano Reggiano cheese
3/4 oz. (20 g) unsalted butter, cut into pieces

Sauté the celery, onion, and carrot in a skillet over medium heat with a drizzle of olive oil and the bay leaf. Once they have turned golden brown, add the ground beef, pork, and the pancetta and cook over medium-high until meat begins to brown. Season with salt and pepper. Stir in the red wine, cook until the wine evaporates completely, then lower the heat and add the tomato paste. Add 2 cups water (or enough water to cover the meat mixture) and cook slowly over low heat for at least 30 minutes. Discard bay leaf.

Meanwhile, prepare the béchamel: Melt the butter in a heavy-bottomed pan. To make a roux, add the flour and whisk butter and flour together for 3 to 4 minutes over low heat, until smooth. Heat the milk in a separate pan, then add to the roux, pouring it in a slow stream. Adjust the salt, season with a bit of nutmeg, and continue cooking, whisking constantly to avoid the formation of lumps, until the sauce is thick and creamy. If the béchamel is too thick, add a bit of milk. If it is too thin, let it cook for a few additional minutes. Heat the oven to 350°F (180°C).

Butter a 9-by-13-inch baking dish and arrange the first layer of spinach egg lasagna lengthwise. Evenly spread a layer of sauce over it, followed by the béchamel and a generous handful of grated Parmigiano Reggiano. Continue to layer the lasagna, sauce, and béchamel until you have used the rest of the ingredients. Finish with the béchamel, a generous dusting of cheese, and a few pieces of butter. Bake the lasagna for 25 to 30 minutes, or until golden brown. Let it rest for 5 minutes before serving.

ALTERNATIVE VERSIONS
For a dish where the bright color of the sauce stands out, make the classic lasagna with yellow egg lasagna sheets.

I ♥ Pasta

MALTAGLIATI WITH SPECK HAM, RADICCHIO, AND BRIE

PREPARATION: 25 minutes
COOKING TIME: 20 minutes
DIFFICULTY: EASY

4 SERVINGS

9 oz. (250 g) Barilla maltagliati
5 oz. (150 g) red radicchio
3 1/2 oz. (100 g) sliced
speck, julienned
2 tbsp. (30 ml) extra-virgin olive oil
1 3/4 oz. (50 g) Brie, diced
1 shallot, peeled
4 sprigs thyme
Salt and pepper to taste

Bring a pot of salted water to a boil for the maltagliati.

Wash and drain the shallot and radicchio thoroughly, then thinly slice.

Heat the oil in a pan over medium and sauté the shallot. Add the speck and cook for a few minutes.

Add the radicchio, season with salt and pepper, and cook, covered, until radicchio is crisp-tender.

Cook the maltagliati in the pot of boiling salted water until it is al dente; drain. Toss pasta with the sauce, add the thyme leaves and the diced brie, and stir to combine.

ALTERNATIVE VERSIONS
Mezze maniche rigate, rigatoni, and farfalle can be used instead of maltagliati in this recipe.

EGG PAGLIA E FIENO WITH FRESH TOMATOES

PREPARATION: 45 minutes
COOKING TIME: 20 minutes
DIFFICULTY: EASY

4 SERVINGS

9 oz. (250 g) Barilla egg paglia e fieno
2 tbsp. (30 ml) extra-virgin olive oil
2 1/4 lb. (1 kg) ripe tomatoes
3 1/2 oz. (100 g) onion, peeled and chopped
1 1/2 oz. (40 g) Parmigiano Reggiano cheese, grated
1 clove garlic
1 bunch basil, coarsely chopped
Salt to taste

Rinse, seed, and dice the tomatoes. Heat the oil in a pan over medium and sauté the onion with the whole garlic clove.

When the onion is golden brown, add the tomatoes, season with salt, and cook for about 10 minutes. Remove the garlic clove from the sauce and add the basil.

Bring a pot of salted water to a boil and cook the pasta until it is al dente; drain.

Toss the pasta with the tomato sauce and sprinkle with Parmigiano Reggiano.

ALTERNATIVE VERSIONS

This versatile sauce goes well with both semolina and egg pastas, both long and short. In terms of semolina pasta, we recommend penne rigate, penne lisce, rigatoni, and spaghetti, and in terms of egg pasta, fettuccine, tagliatelle, and garganelli.

I ♥ Pasta

EGG PAGLIA E FIENO WITH PARMA HAM AND PEAS

PREPARATION: 15 minutes
COOKING TIME: 15 minutes
DIFFICULTY: EASY

4 SERVINGS

9 oz. (250 g) Barilla egg
paglia e fieno
5 1/2 oz. (160 g) peas
5 oz. (140 g) Parma ham,
in one slice
1 oz. (25 g) onion, minced
1/3 cup plus 1 1/2 tbsp. (40 g) grated
Parmigiano Reggiano cheese
1 oz. (30 g) unsalted butter
1/4 cup (50 ml) beef broth
Salt and pepper to taste

Bring a pot of salted water to a boil for the egg paglia e fieno.
Meanwhile, boil the peas in a pan of salted water until crisp-tender.
Cut the Parma ham into strips 1/10 inch (3 mm) thick.

In a pan, melt the butter and slowly sweat the minced onion. Add the
Parma ham and season with salt and pepper. Add a few tablespoons
of beef broth and continue cooking over high heat for 5 minutes, stirring
occasionally. Finally, add the peas.

Cook the egg paglia e fieno pasta in the salted boiling water until
it is al dente. Drain, reserving a few tablespoons of cooking water.
Toss pasta with the sauce. Stir in a little cooking water and the
Parmigiano Reggiano. Serve hot.

ALTERNATIVE VERSIONS
This versatile sauce goes well with fettuccine, tagliatelle, and garganelli.

EGG PAPPARDELLE WITH SAUSAGE AND PEPPERS

PREPARATION: 30 minutes
COOKING TIME: 30 minutes
DIFFICULTY: MEDIUM

4 SERVINGS

9 oz. (250 g) Barilla egg pappardelle
11 oz. (300 g) sausage
3 1/2 oz. (100 g) red bell pepper, seeded and diced
3 1/2 oz. (100 g) yellow bell pepper, seeded and diced
11 oz. (300 g) tomatoes, peeled and chopped
6 1/2 oz. (180 g) onion, peeled and thinly sliced
3 1/2 oz. (100 g) black olives
1/4 cup (60 ml) extra-virgin olive oil
Salt and pepper to taste

Heat 2 tablespoons of oil in a large pan and sauté the onion until it is translucent. Add the peppers.

Remove the sausage casing and crumble the sausage. Heat the remaining 2 tablespoons in a skillet over medium heat and sauté the sausage. When it is well browned, discard the melted fat and transfer the sausage to the peppers. Add the tomatoes, season with salt, and cook for another 15 minutes. Finally, add the olives and a dash of pepper.

Meanwhile, bring a pot of salted water to a boil and cook the egg pappardelle until it is al dente; drain. Toss with the sausage-and-pepper sauce and serve.

ALTERNATIVE VERSIONS

This recipe is excellent with other long egg pastas, such as tagliatelle larghe or pappardelle ricce.

I ♥ Pasta

EGG PAPPARDELLE WITH TURKEY, PORCINI MUSHROOMS, AND BLACK TRUFFLE

PREPARATION: 30 minutes
COOKING TIME: 20 minutes
DIFFICULTY: MEDIUM

4 SERVINGS

9 oz. (250 g) Barilla egg pappardelle
12 oz. (350 g) turkey loin
7 oz. (200 g) porcini mushrooms, cleaned and diced
1/4 cup (50 ml) heavy cream
1 oz. (30 g) black truffles, shaved
2 tbsp. extra-virgin olive oil
Chopped fresh parsley to taste
Salt and pepper to taste

Bring a pot of salted water to a boil for the egg pappardelle. Meanwhile, chop the turkey loin into pieces about 1 1/2 inches (4 cm) long and 1/2 inch (1 cm) wide.

Heat 1 tablespoon of oil in a skillet over medium and brown the turkey. Add the heavy cream and the parsley, season with salt and pepper, and cook for 3 to 4 minutes.

In another pan, heat the remaining 1 tablespoon of oil over high and cook the mushrooms for 3 minutes, stirring constantly. Add mushroom to turkey.

Cook the egg pappardelle in the pot of boiling salted water until it is al dente; drain. Toss pasta with the turkey-and-mushroom sauce, topping with shavings of black truffle.

ALTERNATIVE VERSIONS

Two other egg pastas that go well with this sauce are garganelli and pappardelle. As for semolina pasta, try mezze maniche rigate.

I ♥ Pasta

SPAGHETTI ALLA CHITARRA ALLA GRICIA

PREPARATION: 10 minutes
COOKING TIME: 8 minutes
DIFFICULTY: EASY

4 SERVINGS

12 oz. (350 g) Barilla spaghetti
alla chitarra
9 oz. (250 g) pork jowl (guanciale)
or bacon
1/4 cup (50 ml) extra-virgin olive oil
2/3 cup (60 g) grated
Pecorino Romano cheese
Crushed red chile pepper to taste
Salt and black pepper to taste

Heat the oil in a saucepan and sauté the meat over medium heat for 3 minutes. Add crushed red chile pepper to taste.

Bring a large pot of salted water to a boil and cook the spaghetti until al dente. Drain the pasta and toss it in the pan with the meat.

Sprinkle with grated Pecorino Romano and season with black pepper.

ALTERNATIVE VERSIONS
This classic recipe from Lazio is also excellent with other long pastas, such as bucatini.

EGG TAGLIATELLE BOLOGNESE

PREPARATION: 1 hour
COOKING TIME: 1 hour
DIFFICULTY: MEDIUM

4 SERVINGS

9 oz. (250 g) Barilla egg tagliatelle
3/4 cup (160 ml) water
5 oz. (150 g) pork shoulder, minced
5 oz. (150 g) ground beef
1 1/2 oz. (40 g) carrot,
peeled and minced
1 1/2 oz. (40 g) celery, minced
1 1/2 oz. (40 g) yellow onion,
peeled and minced
1/2 cup (100 ml) extra-virgin
olive oil
5 oz. (150 g) cured pork fat
(or lard), minced
3 1/4 oz. (90 g) tomato purée
1/2 cup (100 ml) red wine
1 3/4 oz. (50 g) Parmigiano
Reggiano cheese, grated
2 fresh bay leaves,
coarsely chopped
Sat and black pepper to taste

ALTERNATIVE VERSIONS

This classic dish from Emilia-
Romagna is ideal with long egg
pasta, such as paglia e fieno
and fettuccine.

Heat the oil in a saucepan over medium heat and sauté the vegetables and bay leaves with the pork fat (or lard).

Add the ground beef and minced pork and raise the heat to medium-high so that it browns well. Pour in the red wine and let it evaporate completely. Reduce the heat to low and add the tomato purée. Season with salt and pepper, add the 3/4 cup (160 ml) water, and cook over low heat for about 45 minutes.

Bring a pot of salted water to a boil and cook the egg tagliatelle until it is al dente; drain.

Transfer pasta to the meat sauce and toss to combine, sprinkling with the Parmigiano Reggiano.

I ♥ Pasta

EGG TAGLIOLINI MONFERRINA-STYLE

PREPARATION: 10 minutes
COOKING TIME: 7 minutes
DIFFICULTY: EASY

4 SERVINGS

9 oz. (250 g) Barilla egg tagliolini
3 1/2 oz. (100 g) unsalted butter
2 sprigs sage
1 sprig rosemary
1 sprig thyme
1 bay leaf (fresh or dried)
1/2 clove garlic
Salt to taste
2/3 cup (60 g) grated Parmigiano
Reggiano cheese (optional)

Rinse and thoroughly dry the bay leaf, rosemary, thyme, and sage. In a pan over low heat, melt the butter and add the herbs with the garlic. After a few minutes, strain the butter with a fine-mesh sieve, discarding the garlic and herbs.

Bring a pot of salted water to a boil and cook the egg tagliolini until it is al dente. Toss pasta with the herb-flavored butter. Sprinkle with Parmigiano Reggiano, if desired.

ALTERNATIVE VERSIONS
This classic recipe from the Monferrato area in Piedmont is also excellent with egg taglierini.

I ♥ Pasta

PARMA HAM TORTELLINI IN CAPON BROTH

PREPARATION: 3 hours
COOKING TIME: 3 hours 15 minutes
DIFFICULTY: EASY

4 SERVINGS

12 oz. (350 g) Barilla
Parma ham tortellini
1/2 capon or chicken
11 oz. (300 g) flank steak, chopped
1 lb. 2 oz. (500 g) beef bones
1 onion
1 celery stalk
1 carrot
1 bunch parsley
1 1/3 gal. (5 l) water
Kosher salt to taste

Place the 1 1/3 gal. (5 l) water and the whole vegetables in a pot with the parsley. Add the flank steak. Thoroughly wash the beef bones and the poultry, then add to the pot.

Cover the pot, bring to a boil, then reduce heat to low and simmer for approximately 3 hours, skimming off the fat from the surface. Add a little kosher salt halfway through cooking. When cooked, strain the broth with a fine strainer and season with more salt, if necessary.

Bring the filtered broth back to a boil in a large pot. Cook the ham tortellini in the broth. Ladle the tortellini and broth into individual serving bowls and serve.

ALTERNATIVE VERSIONS
Capon broth is also great with meat-stuffed cappelletti.

RICOTTA-AND-SPINACH TORTELLONI WITH BUTTER AND SAGE

PREPARATION: 11 minutes
COOKING TIME: 11 minutes
DIFFICULTY: EASY

4 SERVINGS

12 oz. (350 g) Barilla ricotta-and-spinach tortelloni
2 oz. (60 g) unsalted butter
2/3 cup (60 g) grated Parmigiano Reggiano cheese
5-6 fresh sage leaves
Salt to taste

Bring a pot of salted water to a boil and cook the ricotta-and-spinach tortelloni until it is al dente; drain.

Meanwhile, melt the butter in a pan over medium heat and add the sage leaves, stirring to combine.

Transfer pasta to the pan with the sage butter and mix well. Sprinkle with Parmigiano Reggiano and serve.

SOUP PASTA

COMFORT FOOD
PAR EXCELLENCE

Broths and soups, comfort food par excellence, offer welcome relief—a warm caress after a cold winter's day, or a refreshing balm on a hot summer's evening—and the small pasta that traditionally accompanies them are jewels in the crown.

As with all types of pasta, soup pasta comes in many different shapes, sizes, and textures, each suited to a particular sauce. Risoni, for example, inspired by classic rice grains, are exquisite with puréed vegetable sauces. In this chapter you will find two interesting recipes, the first with fava beans and breadcrumbs, and the second with eggplant. Farfalline, a smaller version of farfalle, are ideal with broth or light soups, while ditalini rigati, an age-old Neapolitan pasta shape reminiscent of small open-topped sewing thimbles, are usually served with minestrone, a great classic of Italian cuisine. As for the smooth versions, these are great with legume soups and velvety vegetable soups.

In Italian cuisine, soup pasta is typically used—as the name implies—for first courses requiring a spoon. But there are a few pleasant exceptions, especially with the larger soup pasta shapes, which also lend themselves to dry dishes. Some recipes are enjoyed hot, such as the mezzi canneroni (a smaller version of cannelloni in terms of their cylindrical, smooth appearance), prepared with a delicious lentil, cabbage, and sausage sauce. We suggest serving whole-grain ditaloni rigati with a creamy radicchio and Asiago cheese sauce, as their ridges absorb the sauce to perfection.

Other recipes using soup pasta shapes are for salad, main, and side dishes, and can be enjoyed cold, like the original and delicious stelline topped with diced green apple, raisins, and slivered almonds, or the ditaloni rigati salad with broccolini, chickpeas, and shrimp, a harmonious dish combining the pleasure of vegetables with the full body of legumes and the delicacy of fish.

DITALI LISCI / DITALINI RIGATI / DITALONI RIGATI / DITALONI RIGATI INTEGRALI / MEZZI CANNERONI

MAINLY USED IN SOUPS, *DITALI* GO PARTICULARLY WELL WITH PEAS, LENTILS, BEANS, AND LEGUMES IN GENERAL. *DITALONI* ARE ALSO SUITABLE FOR BAKED DISHES, WITH A MEAT OR VEGETABLE SAUCE AND BÉCHAMEL.

All regions of Italy.

The name, which is evident in the Italian language, derives from the term *ditale*, or "thimble", and is inspired by the pasta's similarity to this sewing implement. This type of pasta comes in different sizes: small, medium, and large. It is also referred to as *tubetti, gnocchetti di ziti,* or *coralli,* In Puglia and Sicily, it also goes by the colorful names of d*enti di vecchia* (old woman's teeth) or *denti di cavallo* (horse teeth).

This is without doubt a historical pasta variety, mentioned in Antonio Viviani's 1824 poem on the "mythical" origins of pasta, Li maccheroni di Napoli *(see quote below), and in the systematic work of Giuseppe Pitré, published in Palermo in 1889 and entitled* Usi, costumi e pregiudizi del popolo siciliano (Customs and Prejudices of the Sicilian People).
Mainly used in minestrone or legume soups, in Calabria they are served ca trimma, *i.e. with a sauce made with beaten eggs, Pecorino cheese, and parsley.*

In 1824, Antonio Viviani (1797–1854), from Lucca, published the playful poem *Li maccheroni di Napoli,* in which he describes Volcano intent on building a wonderful pasta-making machine: the infernal contraption produced the first macaroni, followed by several other pasta varieties, already known and in use at that time:

《 *This class [of pasta] includes Maccheroncini Ditali and Semenze di Mellone, followed by Punte d'Aghi and Stelline, all of which take more than a handful to fill the mouth* 》
From: Viviani, Antonio, *Li maccheroni di Napoli, poema giocoso,* Naples (I), Società Filomatica, 1824.

SHORT, HOLLOW DURUM WHEAT PASTA
Average size by *ditali rigati*:
ength 6.00 mm • diameter 6.15 mm • thickness 1.10 mm
Average size by *ditalini rigati*:
length 5.50 mm • diameter 5.00 mm • thickness 1.00 mm
Average size by *ditaloni integrali*:
length 9.00 mm • diameter 8.80 mm • thickness 1.10 mm

FARFALLINE

THE SMALL VARIETY IS BEST SERVED IN STOCK.

All regions of Italy. Particularly popular in Liguria.

The term is inspired by the wings of a butterfly (or *farfalla* in Italian), which the pasta resembles. This pasta is a smaller, industrially produced version of *farfalla,* and is ideal for soups. It features a single pinch in the middle (as opposed to the double one of the larger *farfalla*), and is called by a variety of names, depending on the size. It is sometimes known as *canestri, canestrini, nastrini, nodini* or *stricchetti* (from a dialect form of the verb stringere, or "to tighten"), referring to the central pinch, or as *galani,* named after the bow-tie worn with a tuxedo, or again as *tripolini,* to mark the Italian colonial adventure in northern Africa (and the Libyan city of Tripoli).

Farfalle *conjure up, both in shape and in the imagination, the graceful multicolored creatures that hover in our gardens. Originally made from thin sheets of dough and pinched by hand, they were once also called* stricchetti. *In 1908, Renato Rovetta, in his* Industria del pastificio o dei maccheroni, *published in several editions by Hoepli, classified a series of pasta shapes cut with a toothed pasta cutter (first and foremost, farfalle), as "pasta a mano uso Bologna." These included* canestrini *and* farfalline, *which were originally prepared with egg. Today, industrial production mostly makes use of durum wheat flour.*

SHORT, PINCHED DURUM WHEAT PASTA MADE FROM A SHEET OF DOUGH
Average size:
length 15.00 mm • width 7.00 mm • thickness 1.10 mm

RISONI

All regions of Italy.

As with the names of many other soup pastas, *risoni* refers to a plant or seed they resemble, in this case, *riso* ("rice").

There are numerous types of soup pastas the shape of which perhaps derived from an attempt to replace real cereal seeds, which peasants used to use to enrich their staple diet composed of soups and broths made with stock and vegetables. Hence, we have risi *(from riso, or "rice"),* lenti *(from lenticchie, or "lentils"),* semi *and* semini *(from semi, or "seeds"),* midolline *(from* midollino, *or "reed"),* all of which, while resembling the true cereals, made cooking and food preparation easier.

DURUM WHEAT PASTA
Average size:
length 9.00 mm • width 1.70 • diameter 2.10 mm

STELLINE

IN MEAT OR VEGETABLE STOCK.

All regions of Italy.

The term clearly refers to the shape of this soup pasta, molded or extruded in the form of stars. In some areas of Italy, the same pasta is also known as astri, fiori di sambuco, stellette.

This star-shaped soup pasta has been known for centuries, a fresh pasta called stelle *having first been recorded in the early sixteenth century by Cristoforo da Messisbugo, carver and kitchen superintendent at the Court of Ferrara. In 1846, Giacinto Carena counted* stelline *among the industrially produced varieties of pasta in his* Vocabolario domestico *(Home Vocabulary).*

Tommaso Garzoni (1549–1589), a skilled sixteenth-century polygrapher, in his unusual and encyclopedic *Piazza Universale*, published in 1585, mentions a long list of Italian pastas, many of which are still used today:

《 *... gnocchi, maccheroni, lasagne, tagliatelle, casatelle, stelle, stellette; and then various kinds of soup pastas....* 》

From: Garzoni, Tommaso, *Piazza universale delle professioni del mondo*, Venice (I), 1585, pp. 297-298.

DURUM WHEAT SOUP PASTA
Average size:
length 1.40 mm • diameter 4.10 mm • internal diameter 0.60 mm

Barilla

DITALI LISCI / SOUP PASTA

LENTIL AND BEAN SOUP WITH DITALI LISCI

PREPARATION: 20 minutes

SOAKING TIME: 12 hours

COOKING TIME: 2 hours 15 minutes

DIFFICULTY: EASY

4 SERVINGS

7 oz. (200 g) Barilla ditali lisci
8 oz. (250 g) mixed dried legumes
(such as lentils, cannellini beans,
peas, fava beans)
7 oz. (200 g) potatoes, peeled
and diced
3 1/2 oz. (80 g) onion, or about 1
medium, peeled and diced
2 1/2 oz. (70 g) celery, or about 3
stalks, diced
2 3/4 oz. (80 g) carrots, or about 1
medium, diced
1/4 cup (60 ml) extra-virgin olive oil
1/2 cup (50 g) grated
Pecorino cheese
Salt and pepper to taste

Soak the legumes in cold water for at least 12 hours.

Heat 2 tablespoons of oil in a pot and sauté all the vegetables for
4 to 5 minutes.

Drain the legumes, add to pot with the vegetables, and cover with cold
water. Bring to a boil, then lower the heat and simmer until the legumes
are tender (one to two hours, with lentils requiring the least cooking
time). Season with salt and add the ditali lisci. Cook pasta directly in the
soup until it is al dente.

To each serving bowl, add a drizzle of olive oil, a sprinkling of Pecorino,
and pepper to taste.

ALTERNATIVE VERSIONS
This soup is also excellent with other
soup pastas, such as conchigliette,
farfalline, and egg lancette.

I ♥ Pasta

DITALINI RIGATI WITH SEAFOOD AND SAFFRON

PREPARATION: 20 minutes

COOKING TIME: 9 minutes

DIFFICULTY: MEDIUM

4 SERVINGS

12 oz. (350 g) Barilla ditalini rigati
8 3/4 oz. (250 g) mussels
8 3/4 oz. (250 g) clams
5 1/2 oz. (160 g) potatoes, peeled
and diced
1/3 cup (60 ml) extra-virgin olive oil
1/2 cup (100 ml) white wine
1 clove garlic
1 fresh bay leaf
1 tbsp. minced fresh parsley
1 sachet of saffron (.0044 oz./125 mg)
Salt and pepper to taste

Thoroughly soak and clean the clams and the mussels (and debeard the mussels), rinsing well to remove all sand and grit. Place the mussels and clams in a pan with the olive oil, bay leaf, whole garlic clove, and the white wine over high heat. Cover and cook until the shells open (discard any mussels and clams that do not open). Remove half of the shells, strain the remaining liquid, return liquid to pan, and dissolve the saffron.

Bring a pot of salted water to a boil and cook the potatoes and the ditalini rigati together until barely al dente; drain. Transfer potatoes and pasta to the pan with the mussels, clams, and their juices to finish cooking.

Add the parsley and toss to combine. Serve with pepper and a drizzle of olive oil.

ALTERNATIVE VERSIONS

The recipe is also great with mini farfalle, gnocchetti sardi, and conchigliette.

I ♥ Pasta

GENOA-STYLE MINESTRONE WITH DITALINI RIGATI

PREPARATION: 30 minutes
COOKING TIME: 30 minutes
DIFFICULTY: EASY

4 SERVINGS

For the soup
5 oz. (150 g) Barilla ditalini rigati
3 1/4 oz. (90 g) leeks, white and light-green parts only
2 1/2 oz. (70 g) celery
7 oz. (200 g) potatoes, peeled
5 oz. (150 g) zucchini
2 3/4 oz. (80 g) carrots
3 1/2 oz. (100 g) fennel
3 1/2 oz. (100 g) bell pepper
3 1/2 oz. (100 g) broccoli florets
3 1/2 oz. (100 g) broccoli Romanesco
3 1/2 oz. (100 g) cauliflower florets
4 Brussels sprouts
1/3 cup (80 ml) extra-virgin olive oil
5 oz. (150 g) Parmigiano Reggiano rind, scraped
8 1/2 cups (2 l) water
Salt to taste

For the pesto
1/2 oz. (15 g) fresh basil leaves, or about 3/4 cup
1/3 cup (30 g) grated Parmigiano Reggiano cheese
1/4 cup (20 g) grated aged Pecorino cheese
1/8 oz. (5 g) pine nuts, or about 1/2 tbsp.
1/2 cup (100 ml) extra-virgin olive oil, preferably from Liguria
1/2 clove garlic
Salt

Bring the 8 ½ cups of water to a boil. Meanwhile, wash and dice all the vegetables.

Heat half the oil in a large pot over medium, add the vegetables, and sauté for 4 to 5 minutes. Add the boiling water and the Parmigiano Reggiano rind and return to a boil, then reduce heat to low and simmer for at least 15 minutes. (Traditionally, minestrone is cooked for longer, but by shortening its cooking time the vegetables will retain a more vivid color and a firmer consistency.) Season with salt and add the ditalini rigati.

Meanwhile, prepare the pesto: Rinse and thoroughly dry the basil. In a food processor or blender, pulse the basil with the oil, a pinch of salt, the garlic, and the pine nuts. Add both cheeses and pulse to combine.

Once the ditalini rigati is cooked (about 9 minutes), remove the pot from heat and let minestrone cool slightly. Serve in individual bowls, topping each with a spoonful of pesto, a drizzle of the remaining olive oil, and a piece of the Parmigiano Reggiano rind.

ALTERNATIVE VERSIONS
Minestrone, a real classic of Italian cuisine, can also be prepared using other pastas, such as farfalline, pipette rigate, and ditaloni rigati.

DITALONI RIGATI SALAD WITH BROCCOLINI, CHICKPEAS, AND SHRIMP

PREPARATION: 45 minutes
COOKING TIME: 11 minutes
DIFFICULTY: MEDIUM

4 SERVINGS

12 oz. (350 g) Barilla ditaloni rigati
8 3/4 oz. (250 g) broccolini
7 oz. (200 g) cooked
chickpeas, drained
12 jumbo shrimp
1/3 cup (80 ml) extra-virgin olive oil
1 clove garlic
1 tsp. chopped fresh parsley
Salt to taste

Bring a pot of salted water to a boil and cook the ditaloni rigati until barely al dente. Drain pasta and rinse with cold running water. Transfer to a large bowl and toss with a drizzle of olive oil so that the pasta does not stick together.

Rinse the broccolini, cut into florets, and blanch in boiling water until crisp-tender. Plunge immediately into a bowl of ice water to stop the cooking process, then drain.

Shell, devein, and rinse the jumbo shrimp, then cut them into bite-size pieces. Sear them in a pan over high heat with 1 tablespoon of olive oil and the whole peeled garlic clove, tossing to cook the shrimp on both sides.

Toss the ditaloni rigati with the shrimp, chickpeas, broccolini, the remaining oil, and the chopped parsley. Season with salt, if necessary.

ALTERNATIVE VERSIONS
This pasta salad can also be prepared with conchiglie rigate, mezze penne rigate, and whole-grain fusilli.

WHOLE-GRAIN DITALONI RIGATI WITH RADICCHIO AND ASIAGO CHEESE

PREPARATION: 30 minutes

COOKING TIME: 15 minutes

DIFFICULTY: EASY

4 SERVINGS

12 oz. (350 g) Barilla whole-grain ditaloni rigati
3 1/2 oz. (100 g) radicchio, finely chopped
10 walnuts, shelled
3 1/2 oz. (100 g) Asiago cheese, diced
1/4 cup (50 ml) heavy cream
1 oz. (30 g) Parmigiano Reggiano cheese, grated
3/4 oz. (20 g) white onion, peeled and minced
1 tbsp. (10 ml) extra-virgin olive oil
4 fresh basil leaves
Salt and pepper to taste

Bring a pot of salted water to a boil for the whole-grain ditaloni rigati.

Meanwhile, heat a frying pan over medium, then add the olive oil and sauté the minced onion for a few minutes.

Add the radicchio and cook for a 5 minutes. Season with salt and pepper.

In a saucepan, heat the heavy cream, and then melt the Asiago, add the Parmigiano Reggiano, and season with salt and pepper. For a smoother cream, blend the mixture in a blender. Keep sauce warm.

Cook the whole-grain ditaloni rigati in the pot of boiling salted water until it is barely al dente; drain. Transfer pasta to the pan with the radicchio to finish cooking. Toss with the walnuts and basil leaves. When ready to serve, transfer the pasta and sauce to a large bowl and pour the Asiago fondue over the top.

ALTERNATIVE VERSIONS
Instead of whole-grain ditaloni rigati, you can use regular ditaloni rigati, conchigliette, or pipette rigate.

I ♥ Pasta

FARFALLINE BROTH
WITH POTATOES

PREPARATION: 30 minutes
COOKING TIME: 3 hours 30 minutes
DIFFICULTY: EASY

4 SERVINGS

11 oz. (300 g) Barilla farfalline
11 oz. (300 g) potatoes, peeled and diced
1/2 capon or chicken
11 oz. (300 g) flank steak
1 lb. 2 oz. (500 g) beef bones
1 onion
1 celery stalk
1 carrot
1 bunch parsley
1 1/3 gal. (5 l) cold water
Coarse salt to taste

Place the 1 1/3 gal. (5 l) water and the whole vegetables (except the potatoes) in a pot with the parsley. Add the flank steak. Thoroughly wash the beef bones and poultry, then add to the pot.

Cover the pot, bring to a boil, then reduce heat to low and simmer for approximately 3 hours, skimming off the fat from the surface. Add a little coarse salt halfway through cooking. When cooked, strain the broth with a fine strainer and season with more salt, if necessary.

Bring the filtered broth back to a boil in a large pot. Add the potatoes to the broth. After about 5 minutes, add the farfalline and cook until it is al dente. Ladle into individual serving bowls and serve.

ALTERNATIVE VERSIONS
This broth is also great with other soup pastas, such as ditalini lisci, egg lancette, and stelline.

MEZZI CANNERONI WITH LENTILS, CABBAGE, AND SAUSAGE

PREPARATION: 1 hour 15 minutes
SOAKING TIME: 12 hours
COOKING TIME: 1 hour 30 minutes
DIFFICULTY: MEDIUM

4 SERVINGS

12 oz. (350 g) Barilla mezzi
canneroni
11 oz. (300 g) sausage
5 oz. (150 g) lentils
5 oz. (150 g) savoy cabbage, sliced
1 oz. (30 g) celery, finely diced
1 oz. (30 g) carrot, finely diced
1 oz. (30 g) onion, peeled and
finely diced
1 cup (200 ml) red wine
1/4 cup (50 ml) extra-virgin olive oil
1 oz. (25 g) sugar
Fresh bay leaf
1 sprig rosemary
Salt

Soak the lentils in cold water for 12 hours. Drain the lentils, then boil them in unsalted water until tender.

In a saucepan, reduce the wine with the sugar over medium heat, until it reaches a syrupy consistency.

Heat the oil in a large pan and sauté the cabbage, celery, carrot, and onion, along with the rosemary and bay leaf.

Remove the sausage casing, then crumble the meat and sauté it in the pan with the vegetables for a few minutes. Add the cooked lentils and mix well. If necessary, add a drop of water to moisten.

Bring a pot of salted water to a boil and cook the mezzi canneroni until it is al dente; drain. Toss pasta with the sauce to combine. Drizzle a few drops of the reduced wine over the top and serve.

ALTERNATIVE VERSIONS
This rustic sauce also goes well with gnocchi, conchiglie rigate, and pipe rigate.

RISONI
WITH FAVA BEAN PURÉE
AND BREADCRUMBS

PREPARATION: 50 minutes

COOKING TIME: 45 minutes

DIFFICULTY: EASY

4 SERVINGS

12 1/2 oz. (350 g) Barilla risoni
1 lb. 2 oz. (500 g) fava beans (fresh
or frozen)
3 1/2 oz. (100 g) onion
3 1/2 oz. (100 g) day-old bread, or
about 1/4 loaf or 2 slices
1/4 cup (50 ml) extra-virgin olive oil
6 cups (1.5 l) vegetable broth, heated
Salt

Clean and chop the onion, then sauté it in a pan with one-third of the olive oil. Add the fava beans, boiled and shelled, and sauté for a few minutes. Then cover with the hot broth. Add salt and let the fava beans cook for about 30 minutes. Once they are done cooking, blend the beans in a blender until they have a thick creamy consistency.

Crumble the bread and toast it in a pan with the remaining oil until it has become crunchy. Meanwhile, cook the risoni directly in the fava bean cream until it is al dente, 8 to 10 minutes.

Serve sprinkled with the toasted breadcrumbs.

ALTERNATIVE VERSIONS

For this recipe, use a cut of pasta suitable for broth soups. As an alternative to risoni, we also recommend egg grattini, midolline, and egg risi.

RISONI
WITH EGGPLANT CREAM SAUCE

PREPARATION: 15 minutes
COOKING TIME: 16 minutes
DIFFICULTY: EASY

4 SERVINGS

11 oz. (300 g) Barilla risoni
2 1/4 lb. (1 kg) eggplant
2 cups (500 ml) vegetable broth
2 tbsp. (30 ml) extra-virgin olive oil
1 bunch basil
Salt and pepper to taste
Vegetable oil for frying (optional)

Peel and coarsely chop the eggplant, reserving some of the peel for garnish.

Cook eggplant in a pot of boiling salted water for about 10 minutes, or until softened; drain.

Transfer the eggplant to a food processor or blender and blend with the broth, the basil, and a pinch of salt and pepper until smooth.

Pour the eggplant cream sauce into a saucepan and cook the risoni directly in the sauce until pasta is al dente, adding some hot water if the sauce thickens too much. Season with salt and pepper to taste. Stir in the olive oil. For a garnish, thinly slice the reserved eggplant peel and fry for a few seconds in hot oil. Serve.

ALTERNATIVE VERSIONS

This recipe goes well with soup pastas, such as midolline and egg grattini.

I ♥ Pasta

STELLINE WITH GREEN APPLE, RAISINS, AND ALMONDS

PREPARATION: 30 minutes
COOKING TIME: 7 minutes
DIFFICULTY: EASY

4 SERVINGS

9 oz. (250 g) Barilla stelline
2 1/2 oz. (70 g) raisins, or about 1/2 cup
3 1/2 oz. (100 g) almonds, or about 3/4 cup
2 tart green apples, such as Granny Smith
1/3 cup (80 ml) extra-virgin olive oil
3/4 oz. (20 g) parsley, chopped
Juice of 1 lemon
Salt and pepper to taste
Slivered almonds, toasted (optional)

Soak the raisins in water for 10 to 15 minutes to rehydrate, then drain well and squeeze out excess liquid.

Wash and slice the apples without peeling them (if you prefer, cut them into cubes) and place them in a bowl with the lemon juice.

Coarsely chop the almonds.

Bring a pot of salted water to a boil and cook the stelline until it is al dente; drain. In a large bowl, toss the pasta with a drizzle of olive oil so that it does not stick together.

Drain the apples, reserving the lemon juice. Stir the apples, raisins, and almonds into the pasta. Using a whisk, emulsify the reserved lemon juice with some salt, pepper, the remaining olive oil, and parsley; then toss the dressing with the pasta. Serve, sprinkling with some toasted slivered almonds, if desired.

This pasta dish can also be served cold.

ALTERNATIVE VERSIONS
This recipe is ideal with tiny pastas, such as ditalini lisci, farfalline, and egg grattini.

I ♥ Pasta

ALPHABETIC INDEX OF RECIPES

ACADEMIA BARILLA
ITALIAN GASTRONOMIC AMBASSADOR TO THE WORLD

Academia Barilla was established in Parma in 2004 with the aim of safeguarding, developing and promoting the most genuine aspects of the Italian regional culture and cuisine. Based on the guiding principle that underlies this prestigious institute's philosophy – that of "food as culture" – Academia Barilla offers food lovers and professional chefs around the globe a fully-rounded overview of Italy, through technical training, high quality products, wine and food experiences, and corporate services. The headquarters in Parma meet all the training needs of the food industry, and are equipped with the multimedia instruments required to host important industry events: in addition to an extraordinary gastronomic auditorium, it includes a restaurant, a multisensory lab and 18 kitchens featuring all the latest technologies. The Gastronomic Library contains more than 11,000 themed books, and an unusual collection of historical menus and culinary art prints: the library's enormous cultural heritage may be accessed via the internet, with hundreds of historical texts now available in digital form. This cutting-edge approach, together with a team of internationally renowned trainers, enable the institute to offer a wide range of courses, meeting the needs of both restaurant professionals and amateur cooking enthusiasts. Academia Barilla also organizes wine and food tours throughout Italy, to give people the opportunity to experience the Italian gastronomic culture to the full.

www.academiabarilla.it

MASSIMO MONTANARI

Professor Montanari teaches Medieval History at the Faculty of Letters and Philosophy of Bologna. From 2000 to 2005 he was director of the Department of Palaeography and Medieval Studies. He has held seminars and conferences in many European countries, Japan, United States, Mexico and Canada. He runs the book series Biblioteca di Storia Agraria Medievale (Library of Medieval Agricultural History) for Cooperativa Libraria Universitaria Editrice, in Bologna. He is a consultant and collaborator of the publishing house Laterza. He is among the founders of the magazine *Food & History*, published by the Institut Européen d'Histoire et des Cultures de l'Alimentation (Tours), which he directed until 2008. He is also a member of the Scientific Committee of IEHCA. He is a member of the Steering Committee of the Italian Center for Medieval Studies in Spoleto. In 1997, together with colleagues from other Italian universities, he founded the Centro di studi per la storia delle campagne e del lavoro contadino (Center of Studies on the history of the countryside and peasant labor), based in Montalcino (Siena), which he also presides. In 2001-2002, at the Faculty of Humanities of the University of Bologna, he instituted a Masters course in the History and Culture of Food, later transformed into a two-year European Masters course, held in collaboration with the Universities of Tours (France) and Barcelona (Spain). For the past twenty years he has directed local and national research groups, on topics related to the history of the countryside and urban settlements, and the relationship between city and countryside.

ALL PHOTOGRAPHS ARE BY ACADEMIA BARILLA EXCEPT THE FOLLOWING:

Ferwulf/123RF: page 62
Svetlana Kolpakova/iStockphoto: page 184
Fuat Kose/iStockphoto: pages 128 and 226
Giancarlo Polacchini/iStockphoto: pages 42 and 95
iStockphoto: page 210
RedHelga/iStockphoto: page 108
Mario Savoia/123RF: pages 270-271
Liubov Shirokova/123RF: page 256
Susan Trigg/iStockphoto: pages 2-3
Fabrizio Troiani/123RF: page 214
Valentyn Volkov/iStockphoto: page 144
Anna-Mari West/123RF: page 198

Original edition © 2013 Edizioni White Star®
is a registered trademark property of De Agostini Libri S.p.A.

The Taunton Press
Inspiration for hands-on living®

The Taunton Press, Inc.
63 South Main Street
PO Box 5506, Newtown, CT 06470-5506
e-mail: tp@taunton.com

Translation: Soget srl

Library of Congress Cataloging-in-Publication data in progress
isbn: 978-1-62710-087-8

Printed in China
10 9 8 7 6 5 4 3 2 1